Biblical Foundations
of
Prophetic Art

Finding Keys in Scripture

Published by Kadosh Art Media
Larnaka, Cyprus

info@kadoshart.media

Image & Design Credits
Cover art and textual images © Jörn Lange. Typeset in Garamond 12.5/15
Typesetting and book design by Richard J Fairhead. richard@rsdt.org
Author portrait by Oliver Pankow, Dortmund, Germany

Publisher's Catalogue-in-Publication data

Author: Lange, Jörn

Title: Biblical Foundations of Prophetic Art: Finding Keys in Scripture

Includes bibliographical references

ISBN: 978-9925-7725-1-3

Subjects: Prophetic art, biblical studies, prophecy

A copy of this title is held at the Cyprus Library

Biblical Foundations of Prophetic Art

Finding Keys in Scripture

Jörn Lange

Contents

To YHWH Elohim
who gave us the keys in His word
to unlock the prophetic depths of the arts

Acknowledgements

I want to thank the Lord, who encouraged me to write this book and carried me through the entire process. I am grateful to my wife, Sheila, who has stood behind me in many projects over the years and released me to take time to write this book and to see it come to pass.

Thank you to the many friends who gave me input, encouraged me and prayed for me during the writing process. Your confidence in me and your reassurance helped me to continue during the difficult phases. I am indebted to my mission leaders in Cyprus and Germany – Jon, Michelle, and Andreas – who were happy for me to write a second book and supported me in taking time out for the project.

Special thanks also go to my proof-readers, Susan, Jen, Sheila and Jerry; to my editor, Martin, and to my image and DTP specialist, Richard – all friends who gladly supported me with their abilities and knowledge. I really appreciate you all!

Introduction

In August 2017, I took part in a 100-hour-long period of worship in an Asian nation. My offering of worship during this time was to paint prophetically and many people came to ask me what I was doing, because they had never seen anything like this before. Over and over again I explained what prophetic art is and where to find it in the Bible. In the following months, people challenged me repeatedly about prophetic art being a modern initiative. Most of them were surprised when I pointed to examples in the Scriptures like the bronze snake, the songs of Deborah and Barak or the prophecies written in the Psalms. Art is more than painting. Writers, singers, composers, dancers, sculptors, designers and people working with fabrics are also artists, to name a few. They can all be prophetic and we can see these arts in the Scriptures.

When friends suggested that I write a book on this topic, I hesitated, unsure whether there would be enough material related to this subject. I thought, maybe I could stretch it to an article? When I started my research, however, it became clear - quite quickly - that there was more than enough material for a book, which you now hold in your hands. This publication is not a scientific work. It is an aid to see how creativity and art are described in the Bible and, where we see prophetic statements and actions in various artistic forms of expression. The footnotes help you look into additional resources if you want to do so. In this book, I intended to introduce people to the topic of prophetic art in the Bible; to challenge people to use the scriptural keys they receive to unlock more of prophetic art for themselves; and, to understand why prophetic artists do what they do.

In the first part of the book, I write about the creative nature of

God, beauty, art and prophecy. I am convinced that everyone who wants to understand prophetic art needs to have a certain grasp of these topics. Creativity, beauty, art and prophecy all work together to influence the identity and purpose of those engaged in prophetic art. Chapter Five contains a discussion of these topics.

In the second part of the book, I look into the Bible and point to various examples of prophetic dance, fabric work, music, painting, sculpture, pottery and writing. Did you know that God the Father, the Holy Spirit and Jesus all sing in the Bible? That all three of them also dance? There were so many moments during my research when I was actually in awe of how the Lord and His actions are described in the Bible creatively.

There are modern techniques like filmmaking or photography which had not been invented in Biblical times. Nonetheless, they can be prophetic and can be subsumed under techniques that existed in scriptural times. One modern art type, installation art, can be seen in the Tabernacle of Moses and even in the table of showbread.

When I thought I was finished, the Lord pointed out another topic to me: prophetic acts. I wondered how prophetic acts might be seen as prophetic art and found this last chapter of the book the most challenging to write. I experienced many revealing moments about prophetic performance and drama during my fact-finding and I believe that you also will have similar experiences as you read the chapter on prophetic action.

Enjoy reading each chapter and evaluate each key for yourself. I pray that you will not only gain information about how to create prophetically, but also insight and wisdom to better grasp your own calling and destiny. God is calling you deeper, and, if you can also help others understand that they are not part of a modern initiative but walk on solid biblical ground, all the better.

Jörn Lange, Larnaka, Cyprus, June 2020

Chapter One: A Creative God

Elohim Creates

'In the beginning Elohim created the heavens and the earth'
(Genesis 1:1, NOG).

This is the beginning of the Old Testament and this is where prophetic art begins. During the early part of my workshops on prophetic art I often ask this question: 'What is the first characteristic of God mentioned in the Bible?' or 'How does God describe Himself?' People give me different answers and all of them describe God, but only a few actually recite Genesis 1:1 and say 'He creates!' If we want to understand prophetic art, we need to first and foremost understand that God begins by describing Himself as a creator.

The Hebrew word in this verse that is translated 'created' is *bara*. It means to create or to make. If we look further into the Old Testament we can see that both *bara* and another Hebrew term, *asah*, are used to describe God's creative actions. In Genesis 2:3, 2:4, 5:1, Isaiah 43:7, and 45:18 both words are used at the same time, God both created and made. When Hebrews describe a person, they usually describe their character or actions rather than their appearance. There are thirteen actions in Genesis 1:1-25 which describe the character of God. Crucially, we are told that every time God created, He did it with His voice, 'Let there be.' Psalm 33:9 reads, 'For he spoke, and it came into being; he commanded and it came into existence' (CSB). This fact is also reflected in the New Testament account of Creation, John 1:3 says that 'All things were made by him,' speaking here of the Word of God, Jesus Christ. Colossians 1:16 says that 'by him [Jesus] and for him all things were created.'

You may have wondered why I selected a Bible translation which uses *Elohim* instead of 'God' at the beginning of this chapter. There are various names used for God in the Old Testament and I think it is significant to understand what this particular name means. The word *Elohim* and its definitions are often discussed among theological scholars. It appears 2,570 times in the canonical collection of Jewish texts, which shows its importance. It is a unique term in Hebrew as it does not occur in any other ancient Semitic language. It is the plural of *El* or *Eloha*, which means 'the strong one'.[1] However, *Elohim* is mainly used with singular adjectives and pronouns and there are two possible explanations why. *Elohim* could be considered to use either what grammarians call a 'plural of majesty or excellence,'[2] which is quite fitting for the One who created the universe, or the word could be interpreted as hinting at the existence of more than one person in the Godhead, describing the Trinity. This name of God could then be interpreted as 'the triune God who created the universe in His might.' This is how God is titled in the beginning and this is how He describes Himself when He gives the Ten Commandments to Moses in Exodus 20:2-3. We are to have no other god before Him.

Another relevant name of God as a creator is YHWH. This is God's covenant name but it is also used often to emphasize His creative power. Nehemiah 9:6 describes YHWH's creative power in detail and Psalm 148:1-5 tells us that this is a reason to praise Him. He is also called the 'one who created Israel' (Isaiah 43:15). This is the God we are dealing with as artists when we create, especially when we prophesy through art and act as His mouthpiece.

Creating is a Process

You might think "Oh, of course, creating is a process! Why state that?" You might note that I did not say creativity is a process. Creativity is never used in the Bible as a noun. This might come as a surprise to some, but God's creative actions are always described through verbs - not nouns. Nouns used in the word field of creating are creator, which is only used for God, not for man, and creation. Even where the term creator is used in an English Bible translation, there is often a grammatical construction in Hebrew which contains a verb rather than a noun. In Job 36:3, the English term my maker actually reads as 'the one contriving of me.' In Isaiah 40:28, the creator is actually the one creating and the list could go on and on. We find the same pattern in the New Testament as well. In Romans 1:25, for instance, God is described as 'the creator who is blessed forever.' The creator actually is a verb form in the Greek, ktizo, not a noun.

Creation is mentioned in three different ways in the Bible which include:

- As an act or point in time: Two words are used for creation in this sense: *katabole* means foundation or conception, seen in Matthew 13:35 and Revelation 17:8 while *ktisis* describes the act of forming or creating, as seen in Mark 10:6 and II Peter 3:4.

- As an outcome or result *Kosmos* means the world as in an orderly arrangement. We see this term in I Corinthians 4:9.

- As the New Creation: In this case, the Greek word *ktisis* is used again with a focus on the process of creating something or someone new. We see this term in II Corinthians 5:17 and in Galatians 6:15.

There are two basic dimensions which typify creative activity in the Bible. One is the composing dimension as in creating the universe, and the other is the performing dimension as in the performing of creative miracles. We do not have the same level as God in the composing dimension, especially as we live as artists after the Fall. We do, however, share in the performance dimension. Jesus said that we would do even greater things than He had done (John 14:12). Igor Stravinsky, the Russian-born composer, pianist and conductor (1882-1971), gave us insight into the way we participate in both dimensions when he said 'mature artists… have an idea and then use the materials available to imagine, embody, or flesh out their intent. In that sense, art is incarnational, just as Christ is God incarnate.'[3] This leads us to the next topic we need to have in our spirit and mind when we create as prophetic artists, which is the fact that we are created in God's image.

In our Image, after our Likeness

Stravinsky phrased his understanding of the process of creating in this way because this is what we are told in Genesis 1:26-27 and 5:1 about humanity. We are created in God's image, *tselem*, and in the likeness of God, *demuth*. Both terms are used in this passage in what is called a 'Hebraism'. This means that two different words are being used to explain the same idea in order to strengthen that idea. The word for image used here, *tselem*, literally means a shadow which is the outline or representation of the original.[4] One could paraphrase the verses from Genesis 1 in the following way: 'And Elohim, the Great Powerful One, filled the man with a representation of himself.'[5] Meister Eckhard, (c. 1260 – c. 1328), a German theologian, philosopher and mystic, described this in a unique way. He said, 'The whole Trinity laughs and gives birth to us. The rhythm of His laughter is the music of the dance of life.'[6]

Tselem corresponds to the Greek *eikon*, which is the term used in the New Testament and the Septuagint, the earliest surviving Greek translation of the Hebrew Scripture, for Jesus as the image of God. II Corinthians 4:4 says that 'Christ … is the image of God.' Colossians 1:13-15 give us more detail, where we read that the Son is the 'image of the invisible God.' Hebrews 1:3 uses a different adjective to explain the relationship between Jesus and the Father. Jesus is 'the brightness of His [the Father's] glory and the *express* image of His person.' What ties these descriptions of Jesus back into the fact that we are created in the image of the triune God is the reality that as followers of Jesus we are being 'conformed to the image of His Son' (Romans 8:29). This means that the reconciliation Jesus bought for us at the cross not only brings us back into the relationship with the Father, but also that the image of God in which we were created is being restored to us and in us.

How then can we outline what it actually means to be created in God's image? Many things have been written about this topic and I will not give you a complete synopsis of the literature. From a human point of view two capacities of humans stand out to me. The first is the capacity to participate in a sacred reality. 'In him we live and move'

(Acts 17:28). The second one is the capacity to love God, to love oneself and others (Deuteronomy 6:4-5, John 13:35). Both capacities were described by Pope Benedikt XVI as the 'capacity for relationship; ... the capacity for God.'[7] This capacity for relationship works both ways. Humans have the capacity to relate to God because He lives in a relationship of three persons in the Godhead and He is the One who wants to relate to people. God is a lover who wants to be pursued (Song of Songs 2:16). God is not unknown, as the Athenians thought (Acts 17:23), but He reveals His name (Exodus 3:14) and He calls man by his name (Isaiah 43:1). When we read the first five books of the Old Testament we see that Israel lived in a relationship with God and life was intended to be a dialogue with God. As artists and especially as prophetic artists, we need to work on the basis that revelation comes from the Lord. If we create from any other source, our art is not prophetic.

The fact that God became incarnate in Jesus as the Word become flesh (John 1:14) shows us that God not only took the initiative to reveal Himself to mankind, but that it is also His initiative to restore mankind back to Himself. God is the One who restores what was robbed - the *imago dei* - at the Fall. This also becomes very clear when we grasp the reality that Jesus makes His disciples 'a habitation of God through the Spirit' (Ephesians 2:22, KJV). Jesus is 'Christ in you, the hope of glory' (Colossians 1:27). It is by God's initiative that every person receives personhood and value, as a being created in God's image, and in His likeness.

God's Poems

The process and the result of being made a habitation of God are described by Paul in his letter to the Ephesians in a very poetic way by writing that, 'We are his workmanship' (Ephesians 2:10). The Greek word translated as workmanship is *poiema*, from which we get the English word poem. Have you ever thought of yourself or of your life as a work of divine poetry or as a work of prophetic poetry? Poetry is concentrated language which wraps a maximum of thought into a minimum of words. Have you ever thought of yourself as a maximum of thought or inner expression compressed into a minimum of words or outer expression?

A poem is also something which expresses form and pattern along with beauty. You express God's form and pattern along with His beauty in human form. The root word of *poiema* is the verb *poieo*, which has quite a few meanings in Greek. The basic meaning is to make, but it can also mean to bring forth, to cause, to fulfil, to ordain, to have purged and to purpose.[8] These meanings give you an impression of the process which underlies the forming of a poem. This is also a description of the process of forming you into the new creation (II Corinthians 5:17), and into God's masterpiece. The process is portrayed in Colossians 3:10 as 'put[ting] on the new [man], which is renewed in knowledge after the image of him that created him' (KJV).

C S Lewis said in *The Problem of Pain* that we are a 'divine work of art.' One could actually paraphrase Ephesians 2:10 as 'We are His work of art.' A work of art, however, be it a painting, a song, a dance, a book, a sculpture or any other creative expression, does not always have easy birth or circumstances. Joni Eareckson Tada, a Christian author, artist and radio personality, describes herself as God's workmanship in her book *A Place of Healing*. She writes:

> *[God] has a plan and purpose for my time on earth. He is the Master Artist or Sculptor, and He is the One Who chooses the tools He will use to perfect His workmanship. What of suffering then? What of illness? What of disability? Am I to tell Him which tools He can use and which tools He can't use in the lifelong task of perfecting me and moulding me into the beautiful image of Jesus? … I am His poem, do I have the right to say, "No, Lord, you need to trim line number two and brighten up lines three and five. They're just a little bit dark." Do I, the poem, the thing being written, know more than the poet?[9]*

In order to understand how God is writing us, how He is sculpting us into His perfect workmanship, and how we can express who He is through our art, we need to look to what He is doing and listen to what He is saying.

Hearing God's Voice

We can listen to what He is saying because He made us in His image. The Hebrew word for listen is *shma*. It does not simply mean to hear, but to hear intelligently or to hear with attention, to hear with obedience.[10] The word has an implied emphasis on obedience. It has a prominent use in Deuteronomy 6:4 which is often described as 'the monotheistic essence of Judaism'[11] as 'Hear, O Israel: The Lord our God, the Lord is one.' This verse is part of a prayer which functions as a highlight of the Jewish prayer services in the morning and evening. The first two words, Hear (O) Israel constitute the title, 'The Shema,' of this prayer.

The entire sixth chapter of Deuteronomy is a summary of 'the commandments, the statutes, and the judgements' (6:1, KJV) which God gave to Israel. God commands Israel to hear, to listen to Him attentively, to 'fear him' (6:2) and to 'observe to do it' (6:3, KJV). Proverbs 3:32 assures us that '[the Lord's] secrets are with the righteous.' This is echoed in John 8:47 as 'Whoever belongs to God hears what God says' and in John 10:27 where Jesus says that 'my sheep hear my voice.'

We need to understand that God is speaking and what He is saying when we hear His voice. We can take several steps in order to learn to distinguish His voice from other voices, such as our own, the voice of other people or the one of the enemy.[12] All these steps are based on Scripture, and include the following:

1. We need to affirm that Jesus is Lord (Romans 10:9-10) and speak it out.

2. Our hearts must be clean before God (Psalm 51:10).

3. We become quiet before the Lord (Isaiah 32:18) so that He can speak to us.

4. Die to self (Galatians 2:20) and give Him everything that could distract you.

5. Resist the devil and he will flee from you (James 4:7).

6. Ask for the Holy Spirit to fill you again and again (Ephesians 5:18) so that He can guide you into all truth (John 16:13).

7. Receive by faith what the Spirit says (James 1:5) and put it into action (James 2:18).

8. Write down the thoughts which come into your mind as Habakkuk (2:2) was told to write down the vision he received.

9. Listen when God brings up passages of Scripture (Psalm 119:105).

Learning to hear God speak is a process. You will go through these steps often. As you do this and become more familiar with the intimate voice of the Lord, you will be better equipped to understand how God is writing you into His poem; how He is sculpting you into His workmanship; and, how to express who He is and what He says through our art.

Important keys in Scripture regarding a creative God:

'In the beginning Elohim created the heavens and the earth' (Genesis 1:1, NOG).

Then God said, "Let us make mankind in our image, in our likeness, so that they may rule over the fish in the sea and the birds in the sky, over the livestock and all the wild animals,[a] and over all the creatures that move along the ground." So God created mankind in his own image, in the image of God he created them; male and female he created them (Genesis 1:26-27).

'For he spoke, and it came into being; he commanded and it came into existence' (Psalm 33:9, CSB).

'All things were made by him' (John 1:3).

'For we are his workmanship, created in Christ Jesus unto good works, which God hath before ordained that we should walk in them' (Ephesians 2:10, KJV).

Chapter Two: Beauty Will Save the World

A Symphony of Beauty

We can see beauty described in manifold ways in the Old Testament. The Hebrew language has many terms which we today translate beauty into English. They all mean slightly different things but together show us that beauty is a characteristic of the God who first and foremost described Himself as the one who creates. Let us look at some of the terms in the Old Testament.

In I Chronicles we are told to 'worship the Lord in the beauty of holiness' (16:29). The term translated as beauty is *hadarah* which means beauty in the sense of honour.[13] The term beauty of holiness is only used four times in the Old Testament. In II Chronicles 20:21, we see Jehoshaphat appointing singers as the Israelites are going into battle against Moab and Ammon to praise the beauty of God's holiness. The singers who proclaim God's beauty are at the forefront of the army and we can see that worship is a spiritual battle! In Psalm 29:2, we are commanded to give God the glory, literally the 'weight,' due His name and in Psalm 69:9, we see that the fear of the Lord, the beginning of all wisdom, is intimately connected to the beauty of holiness.

In Psalm 27:4, King David expresses the deepest desire of his soul, 'to gaze upon the beauty of the Lord.' The term used here in Hebrew is *noam* which means delight or pleasantness.[14] The beauty or delightfulness of the Lord that touches our soul shall 'be upon us' (Psalm 90:17). This is the beauty which lets our innermost being sing and which calls us to be united in our intimate core with the One who created us. In *The Weight of Glory*, C S Lewis phrased this desire for God's beauty by writing,

'We do not want merely to see beauty, though, God knows, even that is bounty enough. We want something else which can hardly be put into words – to be united with the beauty we see, to pass into it, to receive it into ourselves, to bathe in it, to become part of it.'[15]

A closely related term of beauty, *naah*, is used in Isaiah 52:7, 'How lovely [beautiful] on the mountains are the feet of him who brings good news, who announces peace and brings good news of happiness, who announces salvation and says to Zion, Your God reigns.' We see in this passage how beauty is related to Jesus, the one who will bring good news of salvation, and how beauty is connected to governmental authority.

The prophet Isaiah has a lot to say about God's beauty. He describes it in manifold ways and uses three more words to spell out the different aspects of the beauty of the Lord. In Isaiah 4:2, he prophecies that 'the Branch of the Lord will be beautiful and glorious.' He foresees Jesus who is the branch of Jesse (Isaiah 11:1 and 10). The word for beautiful here is *tsebiy*, which means splendour and describes a place of prominence.[16] In 53:2, Isaiah comes back to the 'tender plant,' Jesus, who has 'no beauty that we should desire him' as He suffers for us at the cross. The term used in this case is *mareh* which describes someone's or something's appearance.[17] It comes from a root word meaning to perceive someone or something as so handsome that it is good to gaze upon him, to behold him, or to approve of him. In 33:15-17, Isaiah says that 'he who walks in righteousness' shall 'see the king in his beauty.' Beauty here is *yophiy* which comes from a root word that means to be bright.[18]

We can see that the beauty of God is described in numerous ways in the Old Testament. Psalm 34:8 says, 'Taste and see that the Lord is good.' If we were to see the beauty of the Lord as a fine meal, these would be the ingredients: colour, honour, splendour, governmental authority, spiritual battle, adoration, delight, salvation, prominence and brightness. What a symphony! What an exposition of the character of the Lord! Wayne Grudem defines God's beauty in his Systematic

Theology similarly as the 'attribute of God whereby he is the sum of all desirable qualities.'[19] The Person described in this splendour, as the sum of all desirable qualities, has the power to save the world and to communicate salvation to the world through your art.

Save the World

'Beauty will save the world' is a quote from Fyodor Dostoevsky's novel *The Idiot*. It is spoken by the main character, Prince Myskin, who has epilepsy. He serves as a Christ-like character or 'type' of Christ. If we look at the way God's beauty is described in the Old Testament, we do understand that this Person has the power to save. Is Dostoevsky's statement, then, the utterance of an idiot – or that of a prophet? If we look at Myskin's circumstances in the novel, the one who speaks these words is regarded as a fool because of his sickness. This puts the words into a tension between the beauty which comes from the Lord and the challenges of life's reality which do not reflect this beauty. The reader therefore struggles with perceiving beauty in the midst of pain, a suffering which stems from the results of the fall when 'the beauty of the image of God [was] marred in man.'[20] This can only be redeemed by Jesus' incarnation, death and resurrection.

Jesus did not only bring us back into the right and righteous relationship with His father, He also showed us the beauty of the Lord which shines in Him (Matthew 17:2) and is to shine in us (Philippians 2:15). As early as in Isaiah 4:2 (see above), we are told that Jesus, the branch of the Lord, will be 'beautiful and glorious.' Jesus is described in Hebrews 1:3 as 'being the brightness of [God's] glory.' Jesus is, has and reflects the complete radiance of the Father. The Greek term in this text translated as brightness is *apaugasma*. It comes from a root word which describes a ray of light, a radiance, or even the dawn[21]. *Apaugasma* is a flash of radiance, a beaming forth of radiance, a rhythm of light. We see this pulsing brightness in several other passages in Scripture.

In Ezekiel 1, the prophet describes the brightness, *nogah*, of the glory of the Lord as in a whirlwind, a cloud with fire (1:4) and lightning (1:14). The movement of Jesus' brightness is reflected in the image of the whirlwind which Ezekiel uses to describe what he sees. Above the whirlwind, the living creatures, and the wheels, he sees a firmament and a throne. On the throne is 'the likeness as the appearance of a man' (1:26, KJV). The language used in this passage is the language used to describe the fact that we are made in God's image: likeness is *demuth*, which is the term we have already identified in Genesis 1:26. Appearance is *mareh*, the term used to describe Jesus' beauty in Isaiah 53:2. The man upon this throne is characterized by fire and brightness (1:27, KJV) as well as a rainbow (1:28). What a description of the 'Son of Man [who] sits on his glorious throne' (Matthew 19:28) when all things are renewed.

In Revelation 1:12-16, John turns around to see who is speaking to him.

And when I turned I saw seven lampstands, and among the lampstands was someone like a son of man, dressed in a robe reaching down to his feet and with a golden sash around his chest. The hair on his head was like white wool, as white as snow, and his eyes were like blazing fire. His feet were like bronze glowing in a furnace, and his voice like the sound of rushing waters. In his right hand he held seven stars, and coming out of his mouth was a sharp, double-edged sword. His face was like the sun shining in all its brilliance.

Does this sound familiar? The blazing fire is the translation of *phlego* which means to flash forth. We see the same movement here as in the other passages which describe the beauty of Jesus. John's reaction is 'to [fall] at his feet like dead.' Ezekiel had the same reaction, he 'fell facedown' (1:28).

The same radiance was shown to Peter, James and John on the Mount of Transfiguration (Luke 9:28-36). They portrayed the appearance of Jesus' clothing as 'a flash of lightning' (9:29). The Greek term used here is *exastrapto*, which describes the same pulsing of light we saw in Ezekiel 1, Hebrews 1, and Revelation 1. The result of this brightness is that Peter, James and John want to stay in the presence of this beauty and 'put up three shelters' (9:33). The beauty of Christ draws us into its permanence. It is the glory of God from within (II Corinthians 4:6). The Transfiguration is a testimony of the presence of God which lived in Christ and which now lives in us, as Christ is in us, the hope of glory (Colossians 1:27). It is the same beauty with which Moses' face shone when he returned from speaking with the Lord at Mount Sinai (Exodus 34:29).

The beauty of God portrayed in the Old Testament is the beauty which mankind was created to mirror and to image forth to the world. The beauty of Jesus portrayed in the New Testament is the beauty of the Redeemer who redeems us back into the original image of God. This beauty is living in us, His followers and His artists, and this beauty has the power to display salvation and redemption through our art to those struggling with the challenges of life's reality.

The Beauty of the Redeemer

I would like to talk about one more aspect of the beauty of Jesus as we lay the foundation for understanding how prophetic art, in all its expressions, is the testimony of Jesus (Revelation 19:10). This is the aspect of the beauty of Jesus specifically as the Redeemer. People have called it the beauty of the cross, but I might call it the beauty of Jesus' work on the cross.

The cross was the cruelest way of execution in the Roman Empire. It was a symbol of horror and death. Cicero, the Roman orator and statesman, said 'The cross speaks of that which is so shameful, so horrible, that it should not be mentioned in polite society.'[22] How, then, can something which happened on a cross which was viewed as horrible and not to be mentioned in polite society, become a work of beauty and worthy to be mentioned in polite society? It is the work of Jesus on the cross which brought about this change. It is a work of beauty. Jesus transformed everything He touched and one of the deepest transformations was how we can view the cross on which He died.

In I Corinthians 15:56 (KJV) Paul says, that 'the sting of death is sin.' It took the death of God's son to reconcile us to Him (Romans 5:10) and this act of reconciliation was the purpose for which Jesus came (John 12:27; I John 3:8), a purpose which was given in Jesus before the world began (II Timothy 1:9). Jesus fulfilled the plan and purpose of reconciliation on the cross and changed the way we can view this instrument of horror forever. We have already seen that God's beauty is described in Scripture in a framework of a spiritual battle. The most intense and radical spiritual battle which Jesus fought was His purposed work on the cross. This is the beauty of His work on the cross.

Jesus turned the meaning of the cross upside down. He turned it from an instrument and symbol of death into a symbol of life. This upside-down principle characterizes Jesus' entire kingdom. In John 12:25, Jesus describes this principle in its most basic way: 'He who loves his life will lose it, and he who hates his life in this world will keep it forever.' This speaks of dying to self (Matthew 16:24) and of self-sacrifice. Jesus is the prime example of one who sacrifices Himself for others. He is also the one who gives eternal life, through His sacrifice, to those who follow Him. We have already seen that God's beauty is described in Scripture in a framework of prominence and of governmental authority. The deepest expression of the way Jesus' kingdom here on Earth works is the upside-down principle on which His kingdom is built - a principle of governmental authority which is shown in the work of the cross, leading us back to God's beauty described in Isaiah 52:7.

Within the same passage there is a second illustration of this upside-down way of functioning. Jesus says in John 12:24 that 'a grain of wheat [must] fall into the ground and die, [so that] it brings forth much fruit.' Here we see that death is a tool for new life and multipli-cation. We see the same upside-down principle of self-sacrifice and death leading to something new (life) and beautiful (salvation). The same principle is hidden in the parable of the sower (Matthew 13:1-9). The seed, which is 'the word of the kingdom,' needs to fall into the ground and die (Matthew 13:19). The 'word' in this passage is the Greek *logos*, which not only means word, but also doctrine or princi-ple.[23] Those who receive the principle of the kingdom and *understand* it (13:23) will bring forth fruit a hundredfold, sixtyfold and thirtyfold.

We have already seen that God's beauty is described in Scripture in a framework of the good news of salvation and pleasantness. The one who receives and understands the principle of the kingdom, the good news of salvation coming from the cross, will receive life in abundance and life beyond measure (John 10:10). This life shows itself in multiplying the kingdom (Matthew 13:23). The good news of salvation, which is the news about Jesus' work on the cross brings us back to the loveliness, the multiplication, and the beauty of the One who 'announces salvation' in Isaiah 52:7 - a beauty which King David desired 'to gaze upon all the days of his life' (Psalm 27:4).

Worship the Lord

We have already seen that King Jehoshaphat appointed men to sing to the Lord who should 'praise the beauty of [His] holiness' (II Chronicles 20:21) as they went out before the armies in the battle against Moab and Ammon. The singers, or minstrels, went first in the battle, proclaiming God's beauty by giving honour and adoration to Him and illustrating how we also are called to adore Him in His beauty as we engage in the spiritual battle of worship.

As a little exercise, do an online search for worship songs about the beauty of the Lord. You might be surprised how many there are - and rightly so! If you take a look into the chorus[24] of Tim Hughes' song *Beautiful One* you can see that we are called to adore Him in His beauty as we sing:

> *Beautiful One I love*
> *Beautiful One I adore*
> *Beautiful One my soul must sing*

In the lyrics of the Graham Kendrick song *Come See The Beauty Of The Lord*, the truth of God's beauty is expressed through Jesus' death on the cross. This song describes Jesus work on the cross, the fact that He was slain and takes our blame; and, that His sacrifice has set us free. This act of redemption makes God's beauty visible for Kendrick as 'Come see the beauty of the Lord, Come see the beauty of his face'[25] are the closing lines of his song.

You might have heard the ballad *Beautiful* by *MercyMe*. This song expresses the same truths from a somewhat different angle. It speaks about God as the beautiful One, the One 'more precious of all the earth and skies above.'[26] This picture of beauty is the One who loves us 'madly enough' to die for us. This speaks of the value God gives us through being willing to pay the highest price for redeeming us. This value is the actual spiritual beauty we have, and not our outward appearance, not validation by others, or our accomplishments, as lead singer Bart Millard of *MercyMe* states.[27] The band members have 15 daughters altogether and wrote the song with them in mind. Their value and beauty comes from the One who sees His own beauty in them, because they are created in His image. So much beauty and value that He was willing to die to set them free from the definitions of beauty and value which the world would give them. The list of songs about the beauty of the Lord could go on and on, but I will leave it to you to discover more of the different aspects of God's beauty in these songs for yourself.

Important keys in Scripture regarding beauty:

And when he had consulted with the people, he appointed singers unto the LORD, *and that should praise the beauty of holiness, as they went out before the army, and to say, Praise the* LORD; *for his mercy endureth for ever (II Chronicles 20:21, KJV).*

'One thing I ask from the LORD, *this only do I seek: that I may dwell in the house of the* LORD *all the days of my life, to gaze on the beauty of the* LORD *and to seek him in his temple' (Psalm 27:4).*

'In that day the Branch of the LORD *will be beautiful and glorious, and the fruit of the land will be the pride and glory of the survivors in Israel' (Isaiah 4:2).*

'He grew up before him like a tender shoot, and like a root out of dry ground. He had no beauty or majesty to attract us to him, nothing in his appearance that we should desire him' (Isaiah 53:2).

Chapter Three: Art

The First Work of Art

There are many expressions of art in the Bible. Creation is the first work of art in the Bible, breathed into being by the Spirit of God. God is the first landscape architect. 'The heavens declare the glory of God; and the firmament shows his handiwork. Day unto day utters speech, and night unto night shows knowledge' (Psalm 19:1-2). Ralph Waldo Emerson (1803-1882) said, 'Heaven is the ultimate art exhibition above our heads.'[28] God is the first sculptor. We see sculpture in creation as we look at the creation of the animals and mankind (Genesis 1:20-27). God is the first painter. He puts the rainbow in the sky. 'As the appearance of the bow that is in the cloud in the day of rain, so was the appearance of the brightness round about. This was the appearance of the glory of the LORD' (Ezekiel 1:28). God paints every flower. In Matthew 6:29 Jesus reminds His listeners that 'not even Solomon in all his splendor' was dressed like one of the lilies of the fields. God is the first potter. We see pottery as the sons of Zion are described as earthen vessels, the work of the hands of the potter (Lamentations 4:2). God is the first composer. We see singing as the morning stars sang together at the creation of the earth (Job 38:7).

Also look at art in the Bible *directed* by God. We see carving and engraving in the art in the tabernacle and the temple. We see music and the use of instruments in Davidic worship (I Chronicles 15:16-22). We see song writing as David composes the psalms (II Samuel 23:1) and dancing as He worships the Lord at the entrance of the ark into Jerusalem (II Samuel 6:16). We see fabric art and embroidery in the curtains of the tabernacle and the garments of the high priest.

These are but a few examples of the overwhelming presence of art in the Bible. All these expressions are art. What do they express, then? 'Nothing simple, that is certain.'[29]

The connection between creation and art is very close. The connection between God and art is also very close. Joachim Cardinal Meisner said that it is 'The task and calling of artists to trace the signs of the Creator in the acts of creation.'[30] Artists call what God has hidden in creation and in His word back into the visible realm. Created in the image of God, artists unfold God's creative thoughts as they create paintings, dances, dramas, songs, sculptures, photographs, films, and other works of art, using the reality of God's creation. What they create is an opportunity for the world to get back into touch with its Creator. We will see this specifically in the chapters on fabric art, sculpture, pottery and engraving.

What is Art?

There are as many answers to this question as there are people who have tried to give an answer! Art is 'like a big mirror in which we see the beauty of creation and through which we can infer the glory of the creator.'[31] Art is the process of creating, the original of which we see in Genesis 1 and 2, as well as the results of the creative process, the originals of which we can also see in Genesis 1 and 2. Seth Godin[32] said that 'Art is what we call… the thing an artist does. It's not the medium or the oil or the price or whether it hangs on a wall or you eat it. What matters, [and] what makes it art, is that the person who made it overcame the resistance, ignored the voice of doubt and made something worth making. Something risky. Something human. Art is not in the eye of the beholder. It's in the soul of the artist.'

Art created by human beings, by sons and daughters of the living God, is always based on materials that are already there. The only One who ever created anything *ex nihilo* is the Creator Himself. In this sense, God is the only global artist. There are two aspects to the connection between God and the art we create. One strand is the fact that God created us in His image and the other is that He called us to take care of creation (Genesis 2:15). The process of creating originates in the first strand and the results of the process are part of the second one which leads us back to the Creator. One could illustrate this as a circular movement with the following elements: God as the Creator creating us in His image; artists responding to this fact in creating art, participating in taking care of creation; and, fulfilling the task God gave to humanity by tending to and adding to creation at their own level.

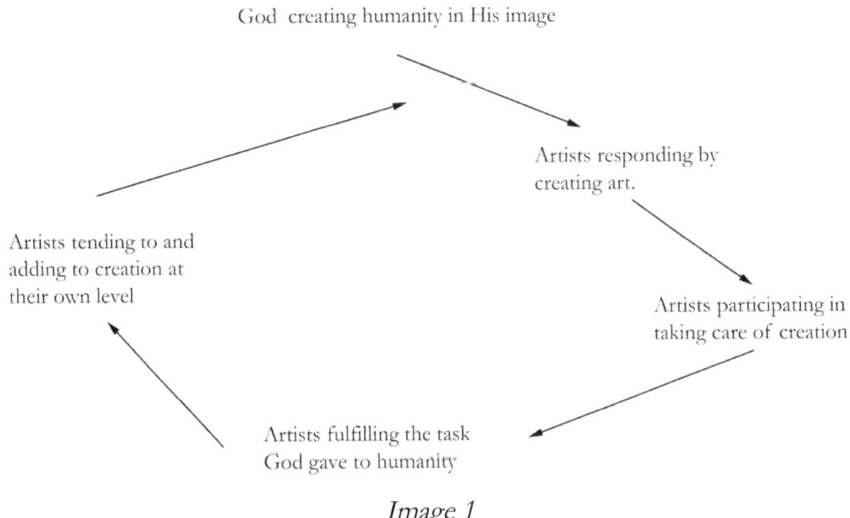

Image 1

The circular Movement of the two Strands

Jeremy Begbie wrote in *Voicing Creation's Praise*,[33] 'Human creativity is supremely about sharing through the Spirit in the creative purposes of the Father as he draws all things to himself through the Son.' It is not a waste of man's time to be creative. Joan Miro, 1893-1983, hinted at being involved in caring for creation while creating works of art when he said, 'I work like a gardener.'[34]

People receive art differently to the way they receive words. When we speak to someone, his or her brain tries to connect what they hear with information that is already there. This means that words face our prejudices, our thoughts, ideas, and our past experiences and feelings. In short, they face everything that our brain has already evaluated and stored. These words are evaluated and possibly rejected according to this information. When people encounter art, they react differently. Art bypasses the mind and goes straight to the heart. This is especially true for images. They are 'multivalent – that is, they have many possible meanings and interpretations.'[35] Art invokes questions as people try to understand what it means. Encountering art allows people to be open to a message to which they might be closed if spoken in words.

This leads us to another question about the definition of art. Is art only art if it calls for a response? Is something which no one can see art? Builders in the Middle Ages created cathedrals and placed works of art high up in the roof or on the facades where no human eye could see them after completion. Legend has it that when asked why they put this art where no one could see it, they answered that God can see these works of art and that they are for Him. True, and even if we do not see the piece of art or hear His response, it is still art.

Art is Incarnational

'The word became flesh and dwelled among us' (John 1:14). The mystery of the incarnation of God is one of the central doctrines in the New Testament. The process is the action of incarnation and Jesus in His human form (Philippians 2:7) is the result of the incarnation. The word, Jesus, whom people had not seen before,[36] was made flesh. The Greek term for flesh, *sarx*, describes something that is visible.[37] Someone invisible and hidden is being made visible. He dwelled among us. Other translations say that Jesus 'tabernacled' among us to express that the Greek term, *skenoo*, means that someone is encamping in or occupying a space, or is residing or communing with someone else.[38] When we create a piece of art, a similar process and result happen. We incarnate or bring into the visible world something that was previously hidden. In the case of prophetic art, we bring a message from God (I Corinthians 12) and deliver it in a visual form. This can be a painting, a dance, a sculpture, a photo or a film, to name just a few artistic expressions. The visualization or piece of art occupies a space, resides with us, and challenges us to interact with it.

This incarnational process, however, does not only go on in prophetic art. To a certain extent it goes on in all art. Every piece of art has a message and often more than one. Every piece of art brings into the visible world something that was hidden before, whether good or bad. This is human nature after the Fall. Bono, the Irish musician and philanthropist, once said in an interview, 'If the job of the prophet is to describe the state of the soul, the soul of the city, if we want to know what's really going on ... you've got to look at the art.'[39] If we want to understand what is going on in society, one way to understand is to look at what is being brought into the open through art. Artists, whether Christian or not, whether prophesying or not, bring messages into the visible world. This is a characteristic of art - it is incarnational.

This message originates in the artist's heart, soul, or spirit. We do not have the space here to unfold a theology of heart, soul, and spirit (Deuteronomy 11:13 and Matthew 22:39). But it has been clear to followers of Jesus through the centuries that artists express messages from these sources. St. Francis of Assisi is quoted to have said 'He who works with his hands is a labourer. He who works with his hands and his head is a craftsman. He who works with his hands, his head and his heart, is an artist.'[40] The heart is the component that distinguishes the labourer and the craftsman from the artist. This is where the Divine chooses to become present and visible and also chooses to 'tabernacle' through colour, brush, sound, movement, pen, stone, form, fabric, and action - if we let Him. We are able to let Him become present because we have the twofold connection to Him in the process and its results. 'After all we *are* an art form.'[41]

Art at the Centre of War

The Bible mentions art and artists many times. We will see significant acknowledgements of art and artists in the Bible when we look at calling, as well as Davidic worship and the Tabernacle of David later in the book. Now I would like to look into art at the centre of war. In II Chronicles 20 we see King Jehoshaphat fighting against the Moabites and the Ammonites. The king knows that he is unable to defeat the vast armies that have come against him. He does what every follower of the Lord should do first, which is he consults with

Him. The Lord answers that Jehoshaphat is not to fight against them, but should simply stand and see the salvation of the Lord with him (verse 17). God tells the king to go out the next day and see God fight. The fact that God tells him to 'stand' reminds me of what Paul writes in Ephesians 6:13, when He tells the Ephesians to put on the whole armour of God and to 'stand' against all evil. When the king and his troops go out the next day, he appoints singers unto the Lord who should do two things: 'praise the beauty of holiness' and 'praise the Lord for His mercy endures forever' (II Chronicles 20:21). We have already seen this beauty in the sense of honour in chapter two. The singers went out in front of the army, according to verse 21. We see how performance art is at the centre of the war here and actually takes first position. This performance art is prophetic since it proclaims the character of God and speaks about Him in the future as 'His mercy endures *forever.*' Now look what happened as the musicians began to sing and to praise. God Himself set ambushes against the enemy armies and they were defeated (Verse 22).

In this case, God used worship in the form of singing to decide the battle. He sent a choir into war! There is another story, actually a prophecy in the Old Testament, which puts artists in the centre of a battle, but this time not musicians and singers. Zechariah saw this prophecy and it is so cryptic that experts have disagreed on a translation to this day. This is what we read in Zechariah 1:18-21:

Then I looked up and there before me were four horns. I asked the angel who was speaking to me, What are these? He answered me, These are the horns that scattered Judah, Israel and Jerusalem. Then the LORD *showed me four craftsmen. I asked, What are these coming to do? He answered, These are the horns that scattered Judah so that no one could raise their head, but the craftsmen have come to terrify them and throw down these horns of the nations who lifted up their horns against the land of Judah to scatter its people.*

Zechariah sees four horns and asks what they are. The angel who speaks with him answers that these horns have scattered Judah, Israel, and Jerusalem. Judah, Israel, and Jerusalem are in a place of war. The next things the prophet sees are four craftsmen. Again, he asks the angel about what he sees, but with a different question. He does not ask what they *are* but what they have come to *do*. The angel describes another stage of war. The four craftsmen have come to throw these horns into panic and to throw down the horns of the foreign nations or Gentiles.

Let us look into the text. The horns, *qeren* in Hebrew, possibly stand for powers and are often interpreted as armies. Armies have scattered Judah, Israel, and Jerusalem. The Hebrew term for the craftsmen in verse 20 of Zechariah 1 is the central term I want us to focus on. The original here is *charashim*, which comes from a root word, *charash*, describing a variety of creative processes using tools.[42] Many English translations of this word make a decision about which type of craftsman is meant in this context. The two main ones are carpenters and smiths. These two create in very different ways and use very different tools. Carpenters are, for instance, named specifically in II Samuel 5:11. The term used here is *charash ets* and clarifies which type of craftsman is meant. Smiths are mentioned, in Jeremiah 24:1, and the term used there is *masger*. Again, it is clear which type of craftsman this is. In my opinion, the context in Zecharaiah is not clear enough to specify which type of craftsman is meant. Young's Literal Translation uses a broader term and simply says 'artisans'.

We can shed further light on the broad meaning of this term when we look into the building of the tabernacle. Two men who are described as *charashim*, Bezalel and Oholiab, built the tabernacle (Exodus 35:35). This broad term is explained further in more detail in this verse as other types of crafts are mentioned, including plaiting, embroidering, weaving, and inventing. The fact that the broad term *charashim* is used first and then further explained, leads me to the conclusion that in Zechariah 1:20, the term also has the *broad* meaning of 'artisans'.

The building of the tabernacle is a unique passage in the Old Testament. It is the first time that artisans are mentioned *and* it is the first time that it says that God 'filled [them] with the spirit of God' (Exodus 31:3). It is actually the only place in the Old Testament where the term 'filled with' in connection with the Spirit of God occurs. The Hebrew word here is *mala* which means to be full of, to flow over, and, to replenish.[43] Moses receives the plans for the tabernacle but Bezalel and Oholiab are responsible for drawing them into the physical realm and building it. They incarnate the message God sent to Moses in their art in the tabernacle. We will look at this occurrence further in Chapter Ten.

Returning to the prophecy of Zechariah, these artisans have come to throw the horns (the armies) into panic and to throw down the armies of the foreign nations (Zechariah 1:21). These artisans, filled with the Holy Spirit and incarnating the messages from God; go ahead in the end times; throw the enemy armies into panic; and, throw them out. Art is again in the centre of war. Could it be that Zechariah actually saw an end-time army of artists? Artists who terrify the enemies of God with 'a clear, brilliant representation of who God is and what heaven is like.'[44] Artists take up their call and enter into the spiritual battle which is already raging. They go first in front of the armies and it will be difficult to defeat them. Their weaponry is manifold - painting, sculpting, dance, song writing, poetry, photography, film, singing, fabric art and other prophetic expressions.

There is an army described in Joel 3:9-12:

Proclaim this among the nations; Prepare war, wake up the mighty men, let all the men of war draw near; let them come up. Beat your plowshares into swords, and your pruning hooks into spears: let the weak say, I am strong. Gather yourselves and come, all you nations, and gather yourselves together all around; cause your mighty ones to come down there, O Jehovah. Let the nations be awakened and come up to the valley of Jehoshaphat; for there I will sit to judge all the nations around.

Here are four points I want to make quickly:

- I have met many artists who think that they are weak, fragile, hesitant, or powerless. 'Let the weak say, I am strong.' God tells you to be strong.

- Artists are called to be part of the Body of Christ and be in community. Gather yourselves together.

- This army is joined by angels, the heavenly hosts, who are commanded by the Lord Himself. 'Cause your mighty ones to come down.'

- Isn't it interesting that God calls the nations to the 'valley of Jehoshaphat'[45] after he has prepared His end-time army? Jehoshaphat sent the choir of Judah into battle!

Just ponder on these things.

Important keys in Scripture regarding art:

'The LORD God took the man and put him in the Garden of Eden to work it and take care of it' (Genesis 2:15).

'See, I have chosen Bezalel son of Uri, the son of Hur, of the tribe of Judah,[3] and I have filled him with the Spirit of God, with wisdom, with understanding, with knowledge and with all kinds of skills' (Exodus 31:2-3).

And when he had consulted with the people, he appointed singers unto the LORD, and that should praise the beauty of holiness, as they went out before the army, and to say, Praise the LORD; for his mercy endureth for ever (II Chronicles 20:21, KJV).

'Wearing a linen ephod, David was dancing before the LORD with all his might, while he and all Israel were bringing up the ark of the LORD with shouts and the sound of trumpets' (II Samuel 6:14-15).

I asked, "What are these coming to do?" He answered, "These are the horns that scattered Judah so that no one could raise their head, but the craftsmen have come to terrify them and throw down these horns of the nations who lifted up their horns against the land of Judah to scatter its people (Zechariah 1:21).

Chapter Four: The Spirit of Prophecy

Foundations

In this chapter, I will give a short overview of prophecy in order to understand prophetic art. Many books have been written on prophecy and you can find some of them in the suggested reading list. What I write about prophecy applies to people operating in their prophetic gift (I Corinthians 14:31). I will not touch on the office of a prophet.

We find the foundations of prophetic art in the foundation of prophecy. God shows us the foundation of prophecy clearly in Revelation 19:10, 'The testimony of Jesus is the Spirit of prophecy.' All prophetic expression, in whatever form, spoken, painted, choreographed, sung, sculpted, filmed or otherwise, comes through the Holy Spirit and glorifies Jesus. We receive it in the river of God which is the Spirit of God. This is the basis and the motivation for all prophecy. Prophetic art is an expression of prophecy – one mode of delivery. For instance, I often use the term visual prophecy when I speak of prophetic painting. God puts this foundation of prophetic expression into a two-fold framework.

First, the angel speaking to John in Revelation precedes God's statement with a command in the same verse, 'worship God,' which ties prophecy back into the first commandment (Matthew 22:37): God is looking for *lovers* who will bring His messages, His Word and Jesus to the people. Secondly, God's statement is spoken as John falls at the angel's feet seeing that 'the marriage of the Lamb is come' (Revelation 19:7, KJV). The marriage of the lamb is the Father's ultimate goal motivated by His love. God links these two defining elements of the foundation of prophecy with each other, worshipping God and being present at the marriage of the Lamb. The important Greek word here is *gar*, found in verse 10, translated as 'for'. It is a small word with a big meaning which is to properly assign a reason.[46] We prophesy in the framework of worshipping God because the marriage of His son has come, and because the Father invites us into a relationship with His son. However we prophesy, we worship God through our creative expressions. The focus is always on Him, not on our creations or us.

The Wedding Feast

We often forget that all divine prophecy is set in the context of the end of time when the final event of history, the marriage of the Lamb to His bride, takes place. His bride is the Church made up out of Jewish and Gentile believers (Ephesians 2:14). His bride is also the New Jerusalem, coming down from heaven (Revelation 21:10) and the tabernacle of God with men, where He will dwell with them (Revelation 21:3) as He did in the garden of Eden. This final event of history brings the entire history of the world in a full circle back to the original intimacy and communion with God. This is where prophecy is based. This is what Jesus died for on the cross, to reconcile us back to God and to restore the beauty of our intimacy with Him.

I have often heard prophetic artists tell me that they partner with God or co-create with Him when they create. This is the position of intimacy that God describes for all of His followers as the position of a bride. God speaks about weddings a few times. In Matthew 22:1-14, Jesus tells the parable of the wedding feast. He says in verse 4 that everything is ready. It would go beyond the scope of this chapter to interpret the parable in its entirety, but it shows the intimacy and honour which God has prepared for the bride of His son.

The prophet Isaiah talks about the same intimacy when he says, 'As the bridegroom rejoices over his bride, so will your God rejoice over you' (Isaiah 62:5). The wedding is a time to rejoice. In the previous verse God says that the land of Zion shall be married and that Israel shall be called Hephzibah, which means 'my delight is in her,' and Beulah, which means to be married. Such is the joy of God at the wedding that He said that He delights in the bride! God delights! John the Baptist saw this delight when He said that the friend of the bridegroom rejoices greatly when he hears the bridegroom's voice especially when the bridegroom comes to take the bride to the wedding (John 3:29). The same delight is the reason that 'a man shall leave his father and mother and be united to his wife and the two of them will be one flesh' (Genesis 2:24). The Hebrew verb used here to describe the relationship between husband and wife is *dabaq* which means to stick and catch by pursuit![47] To catch by pursuit, God is catching sons and daughters by pursuit and uses prophecy to catch them today. He rejoices when He gets them.

Remember, Jesus' first miracle occurred when He turned water into wine at the wedding at Cana (John 2:1-12). He made sure that the festivities could go on after the hosts had run out of wine. What a mundane issue. One thing this shows, however, is the fact that there is rejoicing and celebration at a wedding, as much as there is rejoicing in heaven over one sinner who receives Christ (Luke 15:7). This is the context God chose for the basis of prophecy which is the testimony of Jesus linked to the worship of God.

Prophecy Flows from the Throne

There is another interesting link in this passage. God's voice is described in Revelation 19:6 as sounding like a 'voice of many waters.' Revelation 1:15 and 14:2 say the exact same thing. In the Old Testament we find this phrase in Ezekiel 43:2: '[God's] voice was like the noise of many waters.' Many waters in the Hebrew is *rab mayim*. *Rab* means abundant, overflowing or multiplying.[48] When we paint, sculpt, write, sing, choreograph, dance, or do needlework prophetically, we visualize a message that comes from God, spoken with His abundant, overflowing, multiplying voice.

In Ezekiel 47 and in Revelation 22 we see a river, 'many waters', flowing from the temple and from the throne of God and of the Lamb, respectively. This river is pure, clear as crystal, healing, and life-giving. At the bank of the river is the tree of life which yields fruit twelve times a year. Its leaves are for the healing of the nations. Both in the Old and the New Testament, the descriptions of the river and its impact on the tree(s) are the same. God's voice is pure, like crystal, healing and life-giving. God gives the messages that we receive in prophecy from His throne in purity, clear like crystal they are healing and life giving. Jesus is pure (I Peter 2:22), brilliant like crystal (Ezekiel 1:26-28), healing (Matthew 8:7) and life-giving (John 10:10). Jesus invites us into the river as the angel invited Ezekiel into the river that was too deep to pass. He needed to swim (Ezekiel 47:5-6).

The river of the Spirit is different in certain places and in various times. It can be rushing, as in Jesus cleansing the Temple (John 2:13-17), or slow, as in Jesus going up a mountain to pray alone (Mathew 14:23). It can be deep, as in the seed falling into good soil (Matthew 13:8), or shallow, as in the feeding on milk of new believers (I Corinthians 3:2). The river has islands to rest on, which come directly from Jesus (Matthew 11:28); rocks to sit on, which remind us of God's strength (Psalm 27:5); and, high towers to hide in for protection (Psalm 18:2). It has fortresses on the river's banks where God will guide us (Psalm 31:2); places of refuge for us to flee to (Psalm 62:7); and, broad places alongside where we can build a habitation (Psalm 71:3) and see that God makes room for us (Genesis 26:22). On the river's banks, there are trees which bring fruit (Ezekiel 47:12). The river brings healing (Ezekiel 47:8) and life (47:9). It carries abundance and multiplication (47:9). Such is the flow of God's Spirit that we immerse ourselves in when we visualize prophecy.

The Spirit of prophecy is the testimony of Jesus which *flows* from the throne and the temple. We receive it in the river of the Spirit as we listen to the rushing of many waters - God's voice. The testimony of Jesus, the testimony of what He did for us on the cross, and who He wants to be in our lives, are the messages we bring as we visualize what He shows us.

The River Flows out of Frail Vessels

Jesus promises that out of our innermost being shall flow 'rivers of living water' (John 7:38). I just described this river and Jesus says it will be in us and flow out of us. How does it come out? Paul says in his second letter to the believers in Corinth, that we have the light of the gospel 'in earthen vessels' (4:7, KJV). The adjective used here is *ostrakinos* in Greek, which also means frail. Paul elaborates on this thought in the following verses and describes these frail vessels:

We are hard pressed on every side, but not crushed; perplexed, but not in despair; persecuted, but not abandoned; struck down, but not destroyed. We always carry around in our body the death of Jesus, so that the life of Jesus may also be revealed in our body. For we who are alive are always being given over to death for Jesus' sake, so that his life may also be revealed in our mortal body.

What a description of weakness! Don't we often feel weak, unprepared, unworthy, insecure, tender, low, or vulnerable? We do not have to be perfect before we receive 'Christ in us, the hope of glory' (Colossians 1:27). God works through ordinary, frail people. Even some whom we admire as the heroes of faith in the Old Testament were weak, insecure and vulnerable. Even they came to a point of giving up. Moses was so distressed that he asked the Lord to take his life in Numbers 11:13-15 when the people complained about only having manna to eat. Elijah ran for his life from Jezebel and rested under a juniper tree in the wilderness (I Kings 19:4). There he asked God to take his life as he had had enough. Moreover, remember Jonah who complained to the Lord that He had spared Nineveh. He asked the Lord twice to take his life, once in the city when he realized that God is merciful and that his own prophecy would not be fulfilled because the people had repented (Jonah 4:3). The second time he did this was after the vine that sheltered him withered (Jonah 4:8).

Paul writes that all can prophesy (I Corinthians 14:5 and 31). The prophet Joel foretold this when he wrote that the Lord said that He will 'pour out [His] spirit on all flesh; and your sons and your daughters will prophesy' (Joel 2:28). Peter quoted this prophecy at Pentecost when speaking to the crowd and said that the outpouring of the Holy Spirit at Pentecost was a fulfilment of this prophecy (Acts 2:16).

Why was the Spirit poured out on *these* men and women? They were in the upper room (Acts 1:13) and were together 'in one accord'

(Acts 2:1). The Greek adverb translated as in one accord here is *homothymadon*, a compound word, the second part of which comes from *thymos* which means passion. The root word is a verb, *thyo*, which means to sacrifice. These men and women, 120 in all (Acts 1:15), were in one accord because they were passionate for Jesus and willing to sacrifice their own wills and agendas as well as their own preferences and convictions in order to be of one heart and mind for Him. We see this kind of passion, this kind of willingness to sacrifice, willingness to die to self, also in the passage from Joel 2 that Peter quoted later on that day.

In the second part of verse 28 and in verse 29, God further elaborates the phrase 'all flesh.' He talks about sons and daughters, old men and young men, and male and female servants. He talks about those who are bound to their master. Many times people address Jesus in the New Testament as master, *kathegetes,* which comes from a root verb meaning to lead or to rule.[49] These men and women were the first ones to receive the Spirit because they were willing to bind their entire lives to the Lord. They had enough passion to be willing to sacrifice themselves. The natural consequence was that they were of one heart and mind. Does this mean they were perfect? Far from it. They were still frail, weak and broken, but willing to receive. That all can prophesy is still grace – unmerited favour.

A Cover of Protection

Many people are not used to prophecy. Even more are unfamiliar with the visualization of prophetic words. The same maxims that we would consider when prophesying with words are valid when we prophesy in paint, dance, rhythm, stone, metal, or music. The mode of delivery does not change what God says about prophecy. Let us look at these rules as a cover of protection, both for the one prophesying and for the one receiving a prophetic word.

Prophecy in the New Testament is given to edify, exhort, and comfort (I Corinthians 14:3). This is the natural consequence of the basis for prophecy which is the testimony of Jesus. Jesus came, not to deal with those who are whole, but with those who 'are sick' (Matthew

9:12). The word sick in this passage is the Greek word *echo*. It has a wide range of meanings in various contexts, among them to need amendment; to be diseased; to be possessed; to be fearful; to lack; to tremble; and, to be uncircumcised; ie to be a Gentile.[50] These are the people with whom Jesus came to deal. Do they need edification, exhortation, and comfort? I think so.

As the river flows from frail vessels, we always need to be aware that when we prophesy there will be a measure of our own words, ways of thinking, or processing things. Prophecy, whether written, spoken, or visualized, is always an amalgamation of God's revelation and the way we process it. When we take our first steps in prophesying, we might communicate 20% God's person and 80% ourselves. As we continue to practice and experience the Lord using us, as we receive training and guidance in the process. Gradually we will evolve to 90% God and 10% us. We will grow into giving mature, prophetic words. This is absolutely true for prophetic painting, dance, sculpture, songwriting, photography, or films as well. Paul did comment that prophetic words need to be judged, which helps us in this respect and is part of the protective cover for speaking prophecy (I Corinthians 14:29). Looking at the Greek word for judged, *diakrino*, the passage can also be translated 'let the others discern' or 'let the others reflect.' If we practice this instruction, it has two results. First, we stay humble as prophetic artists and, secondly, we start to see how much of God and how much of us is in what we express. I need to repeat that prophecy according to the New Testament edifies, exhorts, and comforts. I would be very careful in giving a prophetic word, spoken, written, or visualized, as life-changing directives. Also, it is good not to confuse prophecy and godly counsel. If the prophecy has a fine print, we are well advised not to leave it out. God often gives guidance which qualifies an outcome.

How, then, do we act properly in weighing prophecy? Please do not deliver a prophetic word, painting, dance, sculpture, song, or poem in a way that draws improper attention to yourself. Giving a prophetic message is not a matter of flattery. The cover is not there to protect such unnecessary behaviour. The Holy Spirit sometimes might have to remind us that our spirit is obedient, subordinate, or subject to *us* (I Corinthians 14:32). We are not out of control when we prophesy, but in control of our spirit and thus in control of what we say, paint, sculpt, dance, sing, or write. The spirits of the prophets are subject to the prophets.

Prophetic expression always corresponds to the written word of God. The written word of God and the living word of God, Jesus, do not contradict each other. Many times Jesus told His disciples and those who came to hear Him speak that Scripture needs to be fulfilled. Jesus came not to abandon the law, but to fulfil it (Matthew 5:17). The messages we receive need to be weighed against the written word. This is truly independent of the mode of delivery. The unity between the written and the living word is the root out of which a hedge of protection grows.

What about Interpretation?

We can summarize all I have said so far about prophecy under the topic of revelation and where it comes from, how we receive it, and how we deliver it. When I paint prophetically, I sometimes see the interpretation as I finish the painting and hand it to the recipient. Sometimes I do not. Often the recipient's first reaction to a painting is, 'How did you know this?' Well, I did not know - God knew. As it is God's prerogative to determine when He gives a message, to whom He gives it, and what He says in it, so it is His decision to whom and when He gives the interpretation.

Looking at interpretation in the Old and New Testament(s), I would like to point out two passages. In the Old Testament, we see Joseph interpreting Pharaoh's dream (Genesis 41). The Hebrew term for interpret used here is *pathar*. The root meaning of this word is to open up.[51] Joseph opened up the meaning of Pharaoh's dream. His interpretation had immense consequences for Him, for the nation of Egypt and, in the end, also for His own family. He did not take the interpretation of this dream lightly.

In the New Testament, we see Paul describing the interpretation of a tongue as a spiritual gift (I Corinthians 12:30). The Greek term for interpret here is *dimeneuo*. It is a compound word. The first part, *dia*, is a preposition which shows the channel of an act. This means that the person interpreting is a channel of the message - much like the person receiving the prophetic revelation in the first place. The second part, *hermeneuo*, comes from a root word, *ereo* or *rheo*, which means to utter or to give a message.[52] The English word 'hermeneutics' comes from the same root word. The word out of the mouth of God (Matthew 4:4), 'by which man shall live,' is the *rhema*. It also comes from that root word. An interpretation is an utterance or a message which shows the channel of the act. The one who interprets it is part of the act of prophesying.

God can give the interpretation to the one who prophesies. In that case, revelation and interpretation are in one hand. He can give the interpretation to the one who receives the prophecy. In this case, revelation and interpretation are not in one hand. God can also have the person giving the prophecy and the person receiving the prophecy cooperate in its interpretation. Either of these scenarios is fine.

The timing of an interpretation is also important. God can give the interpretation at the same time as He gives the prophecy originally. I sometimes know the interpretation of a painting as I am painting it. God can give the interpretation at the time I deliver the prophecy. Sometimes I do not know the interpretation of a painting while I work on it, but it becomes clear when I hand the painting to the recipient. God can give an interpretation later. I have sometimes painted spontaneous prophecy and handed it to someone who did not know what it meant. I then encouraged the recipient to pray into it. Every now and then I have later been told that they have received the interpretation. A prophecy can be delivered either by the person who received it originally or by a third person. Especially corporate prophesies. For instance, words for church congregations can be delivered to the church by their leadership. A third person can deliver an individual prophecy in specific circumstances to the recipient. I have had paintings delivered to people abroad because I was unable to go abroad myself. God orchestrates each situation in the way He deems best.

One last thought. What about spontaneity? Isn't prophecy spontaneous? Do I receive a word and deliver it immediately to the person concerned? Not always. God can give a word and instruct you to deliver it at a different time. I once created a painting showing a Father throwing his toddler son in the air. I did not know for whom it was intended and stored it in my studio. About two years later when I was on my way abroad to a week-long worship meeting, God told me to pack this painting. On the second-to-last day of the meeting, He showed me a young local man in his twenties and said that the painting was for him. I asked a friend to come with me to interpret from English into the local language, and approached the young man. I explained the painting to him, having received the interpretation at the time of painting, and handed it to him. He broke down in tears, thanked me and withdrew to a quiet place. The next day my interpreter came to me and told me that it had been very difficult for him to interpret what I said. He had known this man from a young age. The young man had lost his father when he was two years old. A local church had taken the family in and helped them survive. That evening when it was time for testimonies, the young man came forward with my painting. He explained the painting and told everybody that God had given him intense healing in his Father relationship the evening before when he received the painting. He closed with the remark that he had been 'reborn' the night before. God knows when to give a message, who it is for, and when to deliver it. Trust Him.

Important keys in Scripture regarding prophecy:

'[God's] voice was like the roar of rushing waters' (Ezekiel 43:2).

The river of God in Ezekiel 47.

'And afterward, I will pour out my Spirit on all people. Your sons and daughters will prophesy, your old men will dream dreams, your young men will see visions (Joel 2:28).

'But the one who prophesies speaks to people for their strengthening, encouraging and comfort' (I Corinthians 14:3).

'For you can all prophesy in turn so that everyone may be instructed and encouraged' (I Corinthians 14:31).

'But we have this treasure in jars of clay to show that this all-surpassing power is from God and not from us' (II Corinthians 4:7).

'For the testimony of Jesus is the spirit of prophecy' (Revelation 19:10).

The river of God in Revelation 22.

Chapter Five: Identity and Purpose

Defining Artists

In the previous chapters we have seen that all expressions of prophetic art are based on the artist cooperating and co-labouring with God. This shared action happens in the position of intimacy that God describes for all of His followers as the position of the bride. The uniting of bride and bridegroom at the wedding feast is the framework for the basis of prophecy, which is the testimony of Jesus. The first four chapters of this book have spoken about who God is, how Scripture describes His beauty, what art is, and describes prophecy. Now it is time to focus on the bride, the human member of this couple, and, specifically, the artists in the bride who co-labour with God. Who does God call them to be? What does God call them to do?

Artists have been defined in many ways. Selecting one definition does not mean that the others are not valid, but this one I believe captures what I think:

> *Our identity as artists is that of sons and daughters, publicly affirmed and sent by the Father to walk as fiery torches of prophetic revelation in the earth while creating from a place of purity and praise in the shadow and protection of God's presence. In that place, we have been given an overflowing impartation of the living breath of God and brought into His intimate presence to be sent as divinely equipped prophetic messengers, carrying His authority.*[53]

In order to better understand this statement, I suggest that you actually write it down on a piece of paper, take some time, withdraw to a quiet place and ask the Lord to speak about the key words in this definition. He will highlight the ones that are most important for you right now. I would also like to suggest that you repeat this exercise a few times while you continue reading this book as He might want to point you to different phrases in the definition at different times. Have fun!

Matt Tommey arrived at this definition having studied the history of Bezalel as it is laid out in the Old Testament. Bezalel is important because it is the first time in the Old Testament that it says that someone is *filled* with the Holy Spirit. We meet Bezalel first in Exodus 31:2-3 where it is written:

> *'See, I have called by name Bezalel, son of Uri, the son of Hur, of the tribe of Judah and I have filled him with the Spirit of God, with wisdom, with understanding, with knowledge and in all manner of craftsmanship.'*

Let us look into these words to establish the stage for what will unfold as we explore Bezalel's calling regarding who he was called to be and what he was called to do.

The word for called here is *qara* in Hebrew. It means that God addressed him by name, He called him out, He invited him, and He proclaimed him publicly.[54] God picked Bezalel out of the crowd for a significant objective. God called Bezalel 'by name'. God only calls someone by name two other times in the Bible. In Exodus 33:19 God says that He will proclaim (*qara*) His name before Moses as He passes him to show him His glory and in Isaiah 43:1, God calls the people of Israel by name and proclaims that they are His. Only three people He calls by name - Bezalel, Himself, and Israel.

Names in the Hebrew culture are important. Bezalel's own name means 'in the shadow of God' or 'under the protection of God.' Other passages speaking about being in the shadow of God include Psalm 91:1, which says 'He who dwells in the shelter [secret place] of the Most High will abide under the shadow of the Almighty.' Bezalel dwelled in the secret place of the Lord (Matthew 6:6). In Psalm 17:8, David prays 'Keep me as the apple of your eye, hide me in the shadow of your wings.' In Psalm 57:1, David proclaims that he will 'take refuge in the shadow of your wings.' The shadow of God is a refuge for Bezalel. Finally in Psalm 63:7, David proclaims that he will 'sing for joy in the shadow of your wings.' Joy bursts into singing as Bezalel lives in the shadow of the Lord.

Bezalel's father's name was Uri, which means fiery one. The name comes from a root word, *ore*, which means to be luminous or to shine.[55] This verb also implies a causative action and in this sense can be translated as to make luminous. Where else is this verb used in the Old Testament? When God led the Israelites in the wilderness, He manifested in a pillar of cloud by day and a pillar of fire by night (Exodus 13:21 and Nehemiah 9:12). The reason for the fire in the night was to give them light in the way they were to take. Light here is *ore* as God Himself gives His people the light they need to find their way. In the well-known passage in Isaiah 60:1, 'Arise, shine, for your light has come, and the glory of the Lord rises upon you.' 'Shine' also is *ore*. The result of the light God gives is that His followers shine in the darkness. Finally, in the Aaronic blessing (Numbers 6:24-26), 'may the Lord make his face shine upon you,' *ore* is also used. Whenever Aaron blessed the people of Israel, God illuminated them with His presence by shining His face upon them. Bezalel's father's name connects to all these meanings. You could say that Bezalel is a son of light (John 12:36).

Bezalel's grandfather's name was Hur, which means white or pure. The family of Hur is also worth investigating. Hur was married to the prophetess Miriam, Moses' sister. He and his brother-in-law Aaron were the two men who held up Moses' arms during the battle against the Amalekites (Exodus 17:12-14). So Bezalel is a grandson of Moses' sister.

Hur was from the tribe of Judah and was actually one of Judah's descendants. Judah means 'celebrated' and comes from the verb *yadah*, which speaks of praising, revering, worshiping and thanking.[56] *Yadah's* root word is *yad*, which is the term for the *open* hand in Hebrew.[57] This root word has a wide range of extended meanings. It describes power, authority, dominion, ministry, strength, as well as fellowship. When

Moses blessed the tribes in Deuteronomy 33:7, he blessed Judah that 'with his own hands he defends his cause.' 'Hands' is *yad* and the word translated as 'defends' actually is *rab*, a term we already encountered when we talked about the voice of God ('many waters'). The translation in the NIV seems to be influenced by ideas not found in the actual text but the KJV stays closer to the text and says 'may his hands be sufficient for him.' In light of the range of meanings of both terms, one could *paraphrase* the blessing as 'may his worship and celebration, his authority and ministry all be abundant, overflowing and multiplying by the myriads.' This is the tribe of Bezalel.

God *filled* Bezalel, *mala*, which meant that he was full to overflowing, satisfied, that he had wholly and was even consecrated![58] God did not describe any of the Old Testament prophets in this way. In their cases, the Spirit of God came *upon* them, but He did not *fill* them. *Mala* is also the verb used in the original mandate to humanity in Genesis 1:28 when God instructs mankind to 'fill the earth.'

God filled Bezalel with His Spirit, the *ruach* of *elohim*, His wind or breath, His life. This foreshadows Pentecost when everyone was filled with the Spirit of God (Acts 2:1-13). Again, the word for God in this passage is *elohim*, the creating one in the plural, which indicates the Trinity (Genesis 1:1). Then God elaborates what the filling with His Spirit gives to Bezalel.

First, he receives wisdom, *chokmah*, which is a wisdom in mind, word, or act. It incorporates a teaching element in its meaning. Second, he receives understanding, *tabun*, which means to be skilful, to discern, to be diligent, and to teach. Even eloquence is in the range of meaning in other contexts. Third, he receives knowledge, *daath*, which comes from the root verb *yada*, to ascertain by seeing. Its translations range from to observe, to advise, to recognise, to teach. This verb is used in Genesis 3:22 to say that Adam and Eve '*know* good and evil' after they ate from the forbidden tree, as well as in Genesis 4:1 when 'Adam *knew* Eve, his wife, and she conceived.' This verb has a connection to intuition, which explains why art bypasses the mind.

We also find all three of these terms in Proverbs 3:19-20 where the Creation of the World is described as

'By wisdom (chokmah) the Lord laid the earth's foundation; by understanding (tabun) he set the heavens in place. By his knowledge (daath) the watery depths were divided, and the clouds let drop the dew.'

God gives Bezalel what He used to create the world!

In addition, all three of these related words have a teaching aspect to them and in Exodus 35:34 it explicitly says that Bezalel taught others. God called Bezalel 'in all manner of workmanship,' *kol melakah*. *Kol* means the whole or the entire range of something. It comes from a root word, which is translated as complete or perfect.[59] *Melakah* expresses 'work' or 'ministry,' but also the products of the labour. Its root verb, *malak*, originally points to 'despatching as a messenger,' which is translated as an angel, prophet, priest, or teacher in various places in the Old Testament.

I suggest that you go through these word meanings again and take some notes asking the Lord to point out characteristics of Bezalel's being and calling. Take some time to retreat and pray about these terms and what they mean for you.

Created for Relationships

What does this tell us? It would go beyond the scope of this book to describe every facet of identity and purpose in Bezalel's life, as others have already done that.[60] I will briefly present three essential lessons from Bezalel's example which are: that God calls artists to an intimate relationship with Him; that God calls artists into community; and that God gives many different expressions and tasks to artists.

God has an intimate relationship with Bezalel. In Exodus 31:2 God says *'I have called…'* He is directly involved in who Bezalel is and what he will do and He is the initiator of this intimacy. Moreover, as said before, God called Bezalel by name. He calls him 'the son of fire in my shadow.' What a description of closeness between him and God!

Bezalel's identity and calling are not individualistic, but corporate. In Exodus 31:6, God explains that He has put Bezalel together with

Oholiab, 'tent of the Father', the son of Ahisamach. Ahisamach is a compound name, the second part of which comes from *samak*. It is translated in various contexts as to sustain, to be steadfast, to uphold, to bind together, and to stay.[61] All of these are descriptions of community. God puts Bezalel together with someone who is called 'the tabernacle of the Father, the son of community.' In this verse, Exodus 31:6, the NIV says 'appointed to help' while the KJV translates it as 'given with him.' The Hebrew phrase here is *nathan eth*. *Nathan* means to assign, to fasten together, to restore, and to shoot forth in various contexts.[62] Bezalel and Oholiab are fastened together and shot forth in the same direction. *Eth* is usually translated as 'with'. The word indicates nearness and comes from a root word which means to meet. In the same verse, God also speaks about other 'craftsmen' as the NIV puts it. These 'craftsmen' are those with skillful or artful hearts. All of them make what God has commanded them to make – together.

When I started to focus exclusively on the ministry of prophetic art at the beginning of 2017, I first worked by myself in loose cooperation with a few other artists. Two years later I joined some other volunteers of Youth With A Mission in our area in a team of seven, five of whom were artists using distinct creative expressions. What a change it was for me as a person and for my calling when this team began to flourish. I understood what it means that God calls artists into community.

God does not limit art to one expression and when I talk about artists, I do not talk about one creative expression exclusively. All people working creatively are artists. In Exodus 31:4-5, we read of metalwork, sculpting, stonecutting, jewelry making, and carving. In verses 7 to 11, we see tent making, fabric art, woodworking, furniture building, weaving, cloth making, fashion design, and perfumery. In Exodus 35, in another description of the construction of the tabernacle, we find architecture and structural building (verse 11), baking (verse 13), candle making (verse 14), spinning (verse 25), engraving, carpentry, masonry, embroidery, and plaiting (all in verse 35). God filled Bezalel with the Holy Spirit to accomplish many forms of creative expression. Is the weaver an artist? Is the woodworker an artist?

Is the architect an artist? Is the fashion designer an artist? Is the jeweler an artist? Yes! Filled with the Holy Spirit and called to make what God tells them to do, all are intended to work together in relationship, not in competition!

Learn to See

There is one more word we need to consider in the light of identity and purpose. Edgar Degas is quoted as saying, 'Art is not what you see, but what you make others see.'[63] As the Lord begins to speak to Moses in Exodus 31:2, His first word is 'see'. The Lord makes Moses see something. A little phrase, *raah* in Hebrew is used over 1,300 times in the Old Testament, literally meaning to see but with a wide range of meanings in different contexts: to approve, to behold, to discern, to mark, to present, to respect, even to spy. God approves of Bezalel and He challenges Moses to discern what He is doing with Bezalel. God has marked Bezalel for a purpose and He presents him to Moses and the congregation. Finally, He challenges Moses to respect Bezalel. *Raah* has many important figurative applications we can identify in the Old Testament.

After God set His rainbow in the clouds as a sign of His covenant of protection with humankind, He said that he will 'look upon' the rainbow and remember the everlasting covenant (Genesis 9:16, KJV). God is reminded of the meaning of the rainbow by 'seeing' it. We can see as artists what things stand for.

When God called Abram, He told him to 'leave your country… and go to the land I will *show* you' (Genesis 12:1). The word translated as show, again is *raah*, to see. In this historic moment and this challenge of trust to Abram, God uses this word to assure Abram that He will show him the way. He does not tell him the final destination, but He confirms to him that he can trust Him. In Genesis 16:13, when Hagar is in the wilderness of Shur, she calls the place where the angel of the Lord speaks to her *el roiy*, 'the God who sees me.' *Roiy* comes from *raah*, which we also read in the second half of the verse.

In the same way, God said to the Israelites that they should go in and possess the land He swore to give to them and their seed

(Deuteronomy 1:8 and 21): 'Behold, ...' He tells them, "see, take notice, this is what I will do."

These are just a few of the many passages in which *raah* appears. God told Moses to see that He is calling Bezalel by name to make what He has commanded. This is exactly how God tells us as artists to see. When we see and when we look at things, we can evaluate things morally; we can know and understand what is going on; we can pay attention to what appears before our eyes; we can understand the signs; we can remember the covenant God made with us; we can trust God; we can understand that God sees us; and, we can see what and how He provides.

These are truths not only applicable to visual artists, but to all creative expressions. Do you understand what is going on as you dance prophetically? Do you pay attention to what appears before your eyes as you sculpt prophetically? Do you remember God's covenant with you as you write prophetically? Do you trust Him as you sing prophetically? Do you see what and how He provides as you organize prophetic events? I think it is time again to retreat. I invite you to read through these appearances of *raah* once more and to ask the Lord to identify some of these particular ways of seeing. Do this and I am convinced you will learn to see in new ways and to understand more of your own identity and calling. Be blessed!

Important keys in Scripture regarding identity and purpose:

'See, I have chosen Bezalel son of Uri, the son of Hur, of the tribe of Judah, ³and I have filled him with the Spirit of God, with wisdom, with understanding, with knowledge and with all kinds of skills' (Exodus 31:2-3).

'Moreover, I have appointed Oholiab son of Ahisamak, of the tribe of Dan, to help him. Also I have given ability to all the skilled workers to make everything I have commanded you' (Exodus 31:6).

Chapter Six: Let Us Dance

Who Created Dance?

I have often heard people ask this question about dance, since it is debated in Christian circles. Let us turn to Scripture as the source of answers to that question, and let us look at John 1:3 where it is written, 'Through him all things were made; without him nothing was made that has been made.' John speaks about God, who is the Word, in the opening passage of his gospel. If God made everything, then God created dance. This is the foundation for the following discussion of this creative expression. The next question people ask is: how to deal with dance? Scripture also answers this inquiry. In Genesis 1:28, God gives the cultural mandate to humankind. We are to manage, lead, guide, cultivate and influence what occurs. We have a responsibility and an invitation to use dance to glorify God and to sanctify it by doing so. This is nothing new, since we are called to do *everything* we do as unto the Lord (Colossians 3:23-24).

In Ecclesiastes 3:4, God proclaims that there is 'a time to dance'. In Psalm 149:3-4 and in 150:4, the psalmist tells us to praise the Lord 'with dance'. The Hebrew word is *machol*,[64] which comes from the word *chul*, meaning to twist, to whirl, to shake, to travail, and to tremble.[65] Isn't there a lot of movement in this word? It also has an implication of birthing something! Take a minute and imagine what our church service would look like if we followed this call to praise the Lord with such intense movements. C S Lewis commented on the Psalms and said: 'The most valuable thing the Psalms do for me is to express the same delight in God which made David dance.'[66]

People have told me that there is no dance in the New Testament. They didn't even ask if dance can be found there, since they were so sure that it could not. Again, let us go to Scripture to find the answer. The first mention of movement in joy, which is dance, in the New Testament is in Luke 1:39-45, when Mary visits Elizabeth, who is pregnant with John the Baptist. Mary arrives at Elizabeth's house, greets and embraces her (verse 40), the unborn baby leaps in her womb 'with joy' (verses 41 and 44). The verb here is *skirtao* which suggests to skip, to jump, and to move.[67] Even the word joy, *agalliasis*, comes from a root word meaning to leap.[68] John leaped with leaps in his mother's womb when she heard the voice of the Saviour's mother.

I have also heard people say, yes, but God never dances. Let us refer to Scripture once again. In Zephaniah 3:17 it says that God the Father will 'rejoice over you with joy,' He will 'joy over you with singing.' To rejoice in Hebrew is *sus*, which means to make mirth.[69] Joy in Hebrew is *giyl*, which means to spin around.[70] It implies intense emotion. Therefore, we might paraphrase this verse in the following way: 'YHWH Elohim will make mirth over you with joy, … He will spin around with intense emotion over you with singing.' Meditate on that for a moment!

Have you ever seen the reference to Jesus' dance in the New Testament? Luke 10:21 says that Jesus was 'full of joy through the Holy Spirit.' The English adjective full is actually a verb in Greek, *agalliao*. It is sometimes translated as Jesus rejoiced. The movement described in the original Greek is usually lost in English, but we can see this movement in the root meaning of this verb: to jump for joy, to leap or to spring up.[71] Therefore, the verse actually says that Jesus jumped or leaped with joy in the Spirit.

We read in Genesis 1:2 that 'the Spirit of God moved upon the face of the waters' (KJV). The word for move here is *rachaph*. It is also translated as to shake or to flutter.[72] The preposition translated as upon implies a downward movement, so we can be sure that the Holy Spirit danced upon the earth at the beginning of creation. We see that God the Father is spinning around in joy; Jesus is jumping for joy and the Holy Spirit is dancing on the waters.

How Does the Bible Describe Dance?

Here is a selection of scriptural keys from the context of the New Testament. In Matthew 5:12, Jesus says: 'be exceedingly glad for great is your reward' (KJV). Be exceedingly glad is the verb *agalliao*, which we already saw above. In Matthew 11:17, Jesus compares His contemporary generation to children who say that people did not dance. The dance word here is *orcheomai*, which describes a circle dance.[73] It implies a regular or choreographed motion. In Luke 15:25, the older son comes to his father's house where people are celebrating the return of his younger brother with dance. The word for dance here is *choros* which also describes dancing in a circle,[74] and is the word from which the English language derives chorus and choreography.

In Acts 3:8, the healed beggar enters the temple 'walking and leaping.' Leaping is *hallomai*. It implies to jump or to gush. The beggar is jumping with joy and gushing with praise in the temple. In Act 6:5, seven people are chosen to serve in the early church. One of them is called *Prochoros*. His name means 'the one who leads in the dance.' Similarly, in Ephesians 5:19 Paul tells the church to 'make melody' in their hearts to the Lord. The Greek verb translated as make melody is *psallo*. Its root meaning is to twitch or to twang.[75]

In Revelation 4:6 and 5:11 there is a preposition which is often overlooked amongst these exciting verses. Both times the English translation is 'round about' (KJV) or 'around.' In Revelation 4:6, four beasts are 'round about the throne' and in Revelation 5:11 there are 'many angels round about the throne.' The prepositions here are two related Greek words, *kuklo* and *kuklothen*, which describe a circular movement and come from a root verb which means to roll about.[76] In this passage, the movement is not implied in a verb, but rather in a preposition. I am not sure whether I would go as far as to say that John saw the multitude of angels dancing around the throne of God, but they were definitely not standing still.

We can see from these short passages that dance movements in the New Testament included jumping and leaping with joy and circle dances. The early Christian church did a lot of circle dancing.

Christian sources in the 2nd and 3rd century AD, described joyful circle dances as one of the 'heavenly joys and part of the adoration of the divinity by the angels and by the saved.'[77]

Have you ever gone carolling around Christmas time? Do you know where the word carol comes from? The word comes from Latin and means to dance and comes from a word that describes a ring or circle. A caroller is a flute player for chorus dancing. Most carols are divided into the *stanza*, which means to halt, and the *chorus*, which means to dance. Next time you go carolling, why don't you invite your fellow singers to dance with you during the choruses?

Now let us look into the Old Testament and point out a few words for dance. In Judges 21, the daughters of Shiloh come out in dances. The Hebrew word here is *chul*, which means to writhe, to whirl, and to dance. The word is used many times in various situations in the Old Testament where motion is described. In Deuteronomy 32:18, the same verb is translated 'formed' as God says that He made Israel. The forming or making of Israel required a lot of motion and God was whirling and dancing when He created her. In Psalm 90:2, Moses used the same verb to say that God created the earth and her inhabitants. Here, we also see that God was dancing and whirling when He made creation. In David's Song of Thanks in I Chronicles 16, he says that all the earth shall fear before God (KJV). Fear is *chul* again, so a more literal translation might be that the earth should tremble and whirl in awe before Him. We also find the same translation of *chul* as fear in Psalm 96:9.

In Psalm 30:11, we read that God has turned the mourning of the writer into 'dancing.' The word used here is *machol*, denoting a circle dance. The dance is the direct result of what God Himself does. We see the verb related to this noun in Exodus 15:20-21 where Miriam and the women 'dance,' *mecholah*. This round dance is combined with antiphonal singing (verse 21).

In I Samuel 2:1, Hannah says that her heart rejoices and that she rejoices after she brings Samuel to the temple. The first rejoice is the Hebrew *alats*, 'to jump for joy.'[78] In I Samuel 30:16, David and his men defeat the Amalekites and are now 'dancing because of all the great spoil they had taken' (KJV). The word used here for dance is *chagag*, which is translated as to move in a circle, to march in sacred procession, to celebrate, or to reel to and fro.[79]

In II Samuel 6:14-17, we see another word for dance as we read that David 'danced before the Lord with all his might.' The Hebrew verb here is *karar*, which means to whirl.[80] This is not a choreographed ring dance, but, rather, movement by an individual executed with intense emotion. I Chronicles 15:29 explains the same movement of King David with a different word. Here the word for dance is *raqad*, meaning to stamp. Moreover, in I Kings 4:31, Machol is named as the father of two of Solomon's officials. His name means dance.

These short passages allow us to see that there was a lot of dance in the Old Testament, including circle dances, jumping for joy, whirling and stamping. Dancing has a long history among the Jews. The founder of Hassidim, one of their groups, taught his followers that 'the dances of the Jew before his Creator are prayers.'[81] He quoted Psalm 35:10, 'My whole being will exclaim: Who is like you, Lord?'[82]

Prophetic Dances in Scripture

When I told a friend who was praying regularly for the writing of this book that my next chapter would concern prophetic dance, he asked a question I've heard many times, 'How can dance be prophetic? Only for the dancer, for the heavenly realm, or to the Lord?' He wanted me to answer these questions. Again, I think we need to start in Scripture to find the appropriate response.

In Exodus 15, the Israelites have crossed the Red Sea and Moses sings a prophetic song (verses 1 to 19). Then his sister Miriam, who is called a 'prophetess' in verse 20, leads the women in a prophetic dance. Only one verse of song is recorded in verse 21 which summarises what God did to save the children of Israel from the Egyptians. In the same verse, Miriam answered them, or responded to them, which shows that there is antiphonal singing going on as they dance. This makes it very clear that the song Miriam sang was longer than the one recorded verse. I believe that she picked up her brother's prophetic song, recorded in verses 1 to 19, and that the sentence in verse 21 is the stanza between the verses. Miriam and the women danced to the prophetic song Moses had sung after they crossed the Red Sea.

In I Samuel 10:5, Samuel tells Saul that he will meet a school of prophets 'coming down from the high place.' They are prophesying in song and music, with lyres, tambourines, flutes, and harps. The Hebrew word for coming down is *yarad*. The word does not simply imply that someone is going from A to B, it implies motion and also means to fall, or to run.[83] The prophets are *in motion* as they make music, sing, and prophesy. What Saul encounters is so intense that 'the Spirit of the Lord will come upon him, he will prophesy and be turned into another man' (verse 6).

In I Samuel 19:20-23, we see Saul on the way to Naioth to seize David who has fled from him. He has sent messengers three times to capture him, but each of them met a school of prophets who were prophesying under Samuel's leadership. As they see the prophets, the Spirit of God comes upon them and they also prophesy, and, of course, do not capture David. So finally, Saul himself is on the way to Naioth and the Spirit of God also comes on him. It says in verse 23 that Saul 'went on and prophesied until he came to Naioth' (KJV). That sounds like a rather calm event. When we look into the original verbs translated as went and came, we see *halak* in the first case and *bo* in the second. *Halak* speaks of running along, moving speedily, and whirling.[84] *Bo* means to besiege, to go into war, and to run.[85] Saul was on a war path and he was whirling and prophesying under the influence of God's Spirit. No wonder this event was worth recording in the chronicles of the time.

Psalm 68 is a song of David about God scattering His enemies. The entire Psalm is a prophetic song, speaking about what God is going to do. Have you heard the song Chris Tomlin, Ed Cash and Jesse Reaves wrote based on this Psalm? It is very war-like and called 'Let God Arise.' In Psalm 68:24, we see God moving in the sanctuary, ie the tabernacle of David. In the KJV the verse is written:

'They have seen thy goings, O God; the goings of my God, my king, in the sanctuary.'

In the NIV, the passage is not much clearer, where it reads:

'Your procession, God, has come into view, the procession of my God and King into the sanctuary.'

The word that confuses me in this verse is the one translated as goings or procession. The Hebrew term here is *haliykah*. It expresses walking, but also a procession or march, and it comes from a root word meaning to step or to whirl.[86] May I suggest that this verse can be translated 'They have seen you moving in steps, O God; they have seen you whirling in the sacred place.' He is a God who dances in the Holy Place to scatter His enemies! The righteous join in this dance as they jump for joy before God in verses 3 and 4. They also remember that in verse 7, God went before His people when he hurled through the wilderness (*tsaad* in Hebrew, usually translated to walk or to march).[87] Verse 16 says that even the hills in which God desires to dwell, leap.

Jeremiah 31:1-30 is a prophecy in which God tells Israel that He will turn their mourning into dancing. In verse 31, God prophecies that the 'virgin' (or bride, ie Israel) shall rejoice in the dance, both young and old together, because He will turn their mourning into joy. Zephaniah 3:14-20 is also a prophecy about Israel's joy and restoration. In verse 17, God says that He will spin over them with joy, *giyl*, in singing.[88] He continues this movement in the next verses when He prophesies that He will gather them, *asaph*. Interestingly, one of the leaders chosen to prophesy with harps, lyres, and cymbals in the Tabernacle was Asaph, who wrote many Psalms. His name means collector and comes from the verb with which God describes His motion as He brings His people back together, gathering them as He spins over them with joy.[89]

Under Your Feet

Dance is a series of movements. We use our entire body when we dance, but the most important body parts in these movements are our feet. We need to briefly look at what God says about our feet to have an adequate idea about what we are doing when we move our feet in dance. For example, as God commissions Joshua in Joshua

1:3, He says that He will give Joshua every place he sets his foot on - a promise originally given to Moses. The Hebrew word for foot is *regel*, which not only means foot, but also step, and comes from a root verb that implies to lead about.[90] As you continue to read the other examples, think about leading with your steps.

In II Samuel 22, David sings a song of deliverance and states in verse 39 that his enemies have fallen under his feet because God had subdued them under David (verse 40, KJV). Subdued in Hebrew is *kara* which describes the motion of bending one's knee. David's song of deliverance is a prophetic song. In Psalm 8:6, David also says that God has put all things under man's feet. He reflects on the cultural mandate that God gave to humankind in Genesis 1:28.

In Isaiah 52:7, we see a prophecy which is often interpreted as pointing to Jesus where it says,

> *'How beautiful on the mountains are the feet of those who bring good news, who proclaim peace, who bring good tidings, who proclaim salvation, who say to Zion, "Your God reigns!"'*

Beautiful in this passage is the Hebrew word *naah*, meaning pleasant, or suitable. Your feet are a suitable tool with which to bring good news, or prophesy in the Spirit giving testimony to Jesus (Revelation 19:10); and they are a pleasant foundation for what you are doing. The same prophecy is stated in Nahum 1:15.

In Romans 16:20, Paul states that God will crush Satan under the believers' feet. This corresponds with David's statement in Psalm 8:6. We see that our feet are a symbol of authority, that we lead about with our steps, and that they are beautiful and suitable signs of good news. This is what you dance with.

Some Practical Thoughts

What posture do we need to have when we dance prophetically? In John 5:19, Jesus says that He can do nothing other than what He sees the Father do. He does what the Father does. We need to express in our movements and in our lives as what we see the Father doing - nothing more or nothing less. Think about what Jesus said in John

14:12, where He tells us that we will do His works as we believe in Him, and even greater ones. What an invitation! What a challenge to obedience and humility! This is the basis of prophetic dance.

This also means that prophetic dance is not a performance. None of the dances or movements we have looked at in Scripture were primarily performances. Even when there were onlookers, such as with the Shulamite's dance in the Song of Songs 6:13, the dance was not a performance but instead an expression of prophecy. People who see prophetic dance need to be drawn in so that they are not spectators. This answers one of my friend's questions: 'Is dance prophetic for the dancer or for the Lord or for whom?' Dance as an expression of worship is communicating a message from people to God. Prophetic dance works the other way around, it is the expression of a message from God to the people. We need to explain this and make it clear before we dance prophetically.

Let us not forget that our body is the temple of the Holy Spirit (I Corinthians 6:19). The Greek word for temple expresses a 'dwelling place.' Our body, which we use in dance, is a dwelling place for the Holy Spirit. We have Christ in us, the hope of glory (Colossians 1:27). How do we move in dance while the Holy Spirit, and Jesus through Him, dwell in us? We must move as living sacrifices (Romans 12:1), holy and acceptable to God. The Greek word for sacrifice here comes from a root verb meaning to be killed.[91] When we bring our body as a living sacrifice, we need to have died to ourselves completely in order to live completely for God. This is the attitude we need to have when we dance prophetically, to convey a message from God to His people.

Dance is an expression in a series of movements. It is very helpful if people understand the meaning of the movements, just as it helps for people to understand the meaning of certain colours in prophetic painting. One thing we can do to draw people into a deeper understanding of prophetic dance is to explain the movements they will see. Some might be readily understood, but others might not. In Appendix 1, you find a list of movements, their meanings, and corresponding Bible verses.

Important keys in Scripture regarding dance:

'Now the earth was formless and empty, darkness was over the surface of the deep, and the Spirit of God was hovering [fluttering, dancing] over the waters (Genesis 1:2).

'Wearing a linen ephod, David was dancing before the Lord with all his might, while he and all Israel were bringing up the ark of the Lord with shouts and the sound of trumpets' (II Samuel 6:14-15).

'Let them praise his name with dancing and make music to him with timbrel and harp' (Psalm 149:3).

'[There is a time for everything], a time to weep and a time to laugh, a time to mourn and a time to dance' (Ecclesiastes 3:4).

The Lord your God is with you, the Mighty Warrior who saves. He will take great delight in you; in his love he will no longer rebuke you, but will rejoice [spin around with intense emotion] over you with singing (Zephaniah 3:17).

'Through him all things were made; without him nothing was made that has been made' (John 1:3).

'At that time Jesus, full of [jumping with] joy through the Holy Spirit, said' (Luke 10:21a).

Chapter Seven: When Fabric speaks

Fabric art can bear the testimony of Jesus and the testimony of Jesus is the spirit of prophecy. We observe several kinds of art in or on fabric in the Old and the New Testaments, including fabric art that portrays spiritual truths, fabric art that someone wears and fabric art that marks physical and spiritual space.

Wearing Art

There is a phrase often heard in Christian circles. It is designated as a 'mantle of prophecy.' It comes from II Kings 2:1-17. A chariot of fire takes Elijah into heaven and his successor, Elisha, had already asked for a double portion of Elijah's spirit to rest upon him when Elijah ascends (verse 9). As Elijah goes up, his mantle falls from him and Elisha picks it up. The 'mantle' is *addereth* in Hebrew. This word comes from a root meaning wide, large, powerful, lordly, noble, or worthy.[92] It says that the mantle fell from Elijah. The word translated as 'fell' is *naphal*, which also speaks of being accepted or throwing something down.[93] This verb carries a causative implication. One could interpret that the mantle did not simply fall from Elijah as he went up, but that Elijah threw it down for Elisha because the Lord had accepted him as Elijah's successor.

Fellow artist, Linde Eller, uses fabrics prophetically. She says that in her ministry to survivors of sexual abuse, the symbol of a cloak, representing God's mantle of protection, features in various ways:

He has sometimes made me offer tangible cloaks to the women I have ministered to. They are unique to each person. He began to prompt me at some point to make pieces of clothing myself, not to use readyßmade ones. These were hand-sewn and hand-painted, a scarf for someone, or a coat for someone else. Each is unique to the wearer and shows a special symbolism according to the words or pictures I was given for that person. Afterwards He inspired me to make multi-coloured coats like Joseph's one. I want to focus on one of these:

Jesus told me to buy a linen cape and write verses of Scripture on it with many different fabric colours. These were arranged to look as if the cape had been sewn together from many pieces, like putting something broken back together again. As the woman for whom I made this encounters Jesus mainly through Scripture, it was very fitting. The cape was to be like a promise or symbol of her inner healing. God's word is what puts her pieces back together again.

When she got the present, something really amazing happened: The weeks or months following, she had a lot of nightmares and severe panic attacks at night. Nothing would help her calm down. When she put on the cape, however she felt Jesus' presence. It was as if arms or wings were wrapped around her, so that she could find consolation and calm down. For a whole summer, at least, the cape ministered relief to her whenever she was suffering from anxiety at night. The soft feel of the cape might have added to that, I suppose, but I really believe Jesus in His grace put an anointing on the cape to convey His sheltering presence to her in a way that nothing else could have accomplished. It humbles me to see how mightily God may choose to use the offerings we give.[94]

For instance, Elijah used his mantle for prophetic acts and signs in II Kings 2:8, and his successor uses it in the same way (II Kings 2:14). As Elisha hits the waters of the Jordan in this verse, he asks the question: 'Where is the Lord God of Elijah?' (KJV) He asks for God Himself. This indicates that he is aware that the prophetic power does not rest in the cloth of the mantle, but comes from the Spirit of the Lord, a double portion of Whom he had already received. Elisha knows that the power is rooted in the relationship with YHWH Elohim. We do well to recognize that the prophetic acts

God does through the mantle of prophecy, as well as the prophetic truths embodied in the high priest's garments, which we will see later, are rooted in the relationship with the One Whose testimony is the spirit of prophecy.

Fellow artist, Flora Chan, shared the following story with me:

I was knitting for homeless people in Auckland, New Zealand, for my first trip there in the winter of 2017. I wanted to knit with colours in the brightest shades possible – just to bring cheer to the downtrodden. I felt compelled a few times to add a black and white neck warmer to the collection. I sort of "protested" because this did not go with my own concept of my collection. Nevertheless, I put it into my bag before flying out. I was helping my friend, a Kiwi missionary who ministers to the poor in his own nation. We went out to the streets to feed and clothe the homeless.

I was giving away my beanies and neck warmers and then we met this tall, young chap. He had been out on the streets for a while and was wearing a beanie and a leather jacket. I asked him if he was keeping warm enough. He said he would like to be warmer around his neck! I dug into my bag and fished out the black and white neck warmer. It matched his entire get up – wow! Holy Spirit knew this moment would happen! I shared with him how I had to include the black and white neck warmer as a gesture of obedience to, and faith in the Lord. I said to him, "Isn't that amazing, that God would send you a woman knitter all the way from sunny Singapore just to show you how much He cares for you and that He was looking out for you?"

We took a picture of him wearing my knitted neck warmer and my friend posted the picture on Facebook. We managed to locate his sister who had no idea her brother was living on the streets. So that was a happy ending.[95]

Brian Mills, senior advisor in the International Prayer Council and one of the leaders in the International Reconciliation Movement, shared a story about a white scarf in our School of Intercessory Prayer.[96] When he was getting ready to travel to Australia to meet with leaders of the aborigines, he asked the Lord what to pack. God told him to pack a white shawl. He thought that he did not need a shawl because it would be hot anyway, but he was obedient. After he had arrived in Australia, God told him to wear the shawl when he was going to a specific meeting with the leaders. That day, reconciliation on behalf of the British people and the aborigines happened. The leaders asked him if he knew what the white shawl meant in their culture and he said no. The white shawl is a sign of mourning. The fact that he wore this shawl meant that the leaders opened up and were willing to associate with him. Later they anointed the shawl with oil and used it to pray over the land.

Portraying Spiritual Truths

Fabric can not just be worn prophetically but can be used in other ways. In the Old Testament, there is also fabric art which portrays spiritual truths, specifically banners. In Exodus 17:15, Moses built an altar after the Israelites defeated Amalek. He calls the altar *YHWH nissiy*, which means 'God is my banner.' The second part comes from *nes*, a Hebrew words speaking of shimmering from afar or fluttering in the wind.[97] God Himself is described as a banner in this passage. The victory over Amalek was achieved because Aaron, Moses' brother, and Hur, his brother-in-law, held up Moses' arms in prayer during the battle. The name of the altar embodies the fact that Moses' arms were lifted up like a banner and that God brought the victory and thus is a banner over His people.

The prophet Isaiah also calls Jesus a banner in chapter 11 verse 10, where he says that the root of Jesse shall be 'a banner to the people' and that the Gentiles shall come to him. He makes a similar point in 49:22 where he also speaks about Jesus as a banner. This is the context for the well-known statement that God will bring back Israel's sons in the Gentiles' arms and that the Gentiles will carry Israel's daughters back on their shoulders. Song of Songs 2:4 says that God's banner over the beloved is love. The word for banner used here is *degel*. It comes from a root word which means to raise up.[98] Jesus prophesied that He would be lifted up (John 12:32) and that He will draw all to Him. He spoke about His work on the cross.

If we look into Scripture for more keys about banners and what they portray, we can find four main spiritual or prophetic meanings of banners:[99]

1. Banners proclaim an event or a truth. The prophet Jeremiah says to lift up a banner to proclaim that Babylon is fallen (Jeremiah 50:2). He later commands that a banner be raised to mark the fact that God is going to do against Babylon what He has already proclaimed (51:12). These banners visualize truths which we need to proclaim. We can use banners to make scriptural truths visible and to proclaim them prophetically over situations, places or peoples.

2. Banners signify hope and symbolize victory. In Psalm 20:5, David says that the Israelites will rejoice or sing because of their salvation and will raise up banners in the name of their God as He fulfills all their petitions.

3. Banners show the way. In Isaiah 7:14, the prophet speaks of the sign of Immanuel: 'A virgin shall conceive and bear a son, and shall call his name Immanuel' (KJV). The word for sign, *oth*, also means a flag which appears.[100] God will have a flag appear in the fact that God will be with us in the form of Jesus, born to a virgin. In Isaiah 62:10-11, we also find another prophetic foretelling of Jesus and another prophecy that a banner will be lifted to show the way and to point to Jesus:

Pass through, pass through the gates! Prepare the way of the people. Build up, build up the highway! Remove the stones. Raise a banner for the nations. The Lord has made proclamation to the ends of the earth: "Say to daughter Zion, "See, your Saviour comes! See, his reward is with him, and his recompense accompanies him."

4. Banners offer protection and security. In Psalm 60:4-5, David says that God has given a banner to those who fear him and that it will be displayed to signify the truth. There are three consequences

for those who rally to the banner (verse 5): they will be delivered, they will be saved, and they will hear Him. We see that God the Father and Jesus are both called banners. Their sign over us is love and their banners proclaim truth, signify hope and victory, show the way, and call us to come under protection and security.

Wearing Prophecy

Let us now turn to a powerful example of people wearing prophecy in the Old Testament. When God spoke to Moses about the creation of the tabernacle, He spoke about the high priest wearing art. The entire Chapter 28 in the book of Exodus describes the priest's garments. These garments are described in several ways: they are holy (verse 2); they are for glory and beauty (verse 2); they are for Aaron's consecration (verse 3); and, he is to wear them ministering to God (verse 3). I will focus on the prophetic meaning of these garments as we can see it now from the New Covenant point of view. The eight garments of the high priest are an ephod (verses 5-14), a breastplate (verses 15-30), shoulder stones (verses 9-12), a robe (verses 31-35), a tunic or coat (verse 39), a turban (verse 39), a gold plate (verses 36-38), and breeches (verse 42).

The craftsmen who are to make these garments are called 'wise hearted' in verse 3, translated from *chakam leb*. The identical description is used of the craftsmen in Exodus 31:6. God sent Oholiab and these artisans to Bezalel to make everything that He had commanded them to make, including the priest's garments. Then the children of Israel gave all the materials for the tabernacle, including the garments, as sacrifices (Exodus 25:1-9).

The Ephod

The ephod of the priest was made with gold, with blue, purple and scarlet yarn, and with fine linen. In Biblical times four colours of cloth were produced by dyeing – purple, blue, scarlet, and crimson. Let us look into the prophetic meaning of these colours. For instance, Gold stands for holiness (Exodus 28:36), purity (Revelation 3:18), and testing (Job 23:10). Blue stands for the Holy Spirit (John 7:37-39 and

Revelation 22:17). Purple represents royalty (Esther 8:15). Scarlet or red carries a whole range of meanings. It signifies cleansing (Leviticus 14:4 and 52), the Covenant (Exodus 24:8 and Matthew 26:28), forgiveness (Hebrews 9:22), the Passover (Exodus 12:13), and salvation (Joshua 2:17-21). Red is also the meaning of the name Adam, the first man, as he was made from the red soil. Thus, red points both to the first Adam and to the second Adam, Jesus. Blue and red combine to make purple, reinforcing the royalty of Jesus as portrayed in the ephod.

The ephod of the priest was made with fine linen. The Hebrew word applicable here is *shesh*, which comes from a root verb expressing the process of bleaching.[101] It is sometimes translated as 'byssus' and was probably made from a type of flax or hemp. In Revelation 19:8, fine linen is called *bussinos* in Greek, which 'is the righteousness of saints' (KJV). The armies of heaven who follow the rider on the white horse in Revelation 19:14 are also dressed in fine linen. The priest's ephod described in Exodus was like an apron and went from below the rib cage all the way down to the ground.

The Breastplate

The breastplate was the second of the garments. It is called the 'breastplate of judgement' in Exodus 28:15 (KJV) because it contained the *urim* and the *thummim* which were used to receive answers from the Lord. The breastplate was doubled over (verse 16) so that it formed a pouch where the *urim* and *thummim* were carried all the time, while Aaron wore the plate. It was also made from gold, blue, purple and scarlet yarn, from fine linen (verse 15) and contained four rows of three precious stones each (verses 17-21). The names of the twelve tribes of Israel were engraved on them. Aaron wore these gems over his heart (verse 29). This position points towards Jesus' eternal love for His people (John 13:1). The gemstones were a reminder of the tribes of Israel to the Lord (verse 29) and an interesting little word in this verse, *paniym*, which is often translated as before, gives us more detail. Its essential meaning is a face. Aaron wore the names of the tribes of Israel over his heart in order to bring them in front of the face of God. In I Kings 13:6, the word is actually translated as the face of God and it is in the context of asking an answer from the Lord.

We do not really know the exact identity of each of these stones. Many people have tried to define each one and then to give each a symbolic or prophetic meaning. Instead, I would like to look into four verses from Scripture to find keys to the meaning of precious. In Isaiah 28:16, God says that He will lay a corner stone in Zion, a sure foundation, a precious stone, which is Jesus. I Peter 2:6 quotes this prophecy. In Isaiah 54:11-12, God prophesies that He is going to build Israel's foundations, windows and gates with precious stones.

In Malachi 3:16-18, God speaks of the ones that fear Him and that their names are written in the book of remembrance (3:16). God calls them His own (verse 17) and He also calls them His jewels (verse 17). The term remembrance is the same word as in Exodus 28:29, *zikron*. The book of remembrance and the book of life (Revelation 20:12) are the same book. Revelation 21:11 says that the light of the New Jerusalem is like the light of a precious stone. The light of this city is the glory of God and the lamb of God (verse 23). In verses 19 and 20 it also says that the foundation of the city walls was made from twelve precious stones. People have tried to correlate these 12 stones with the ones on Aaron's breastplate, but it is difficult to do, as those stones are hard to identify. I would not be surprised, however, if such a correlation exists.

We also see that Jesus is called a precious stone, that His followers are called precious stones; that the foundations of Zion, both in the Old Testament (Israel or Jerusalem) and in the New Testament (the church full of messianic and Gentile believers), are made of precious stones.

The Shoulder Stones

The shoulder stones are the third part of the garments. They are two precious stones, most likely beryl or onyx, set on Aaron's shoulders and also engraved with the names of Israel. Aaron wore them as a reminder before the Lord. The names were engraved in their birth order while on the breastplate, they might have been in their marching order.

The Robe

The robe was the fourth piece of the garments. It was an outer garment in blue, representing the Holy Spirit. The hem of the robe had blue, purple, and scarlet pomegranates, symbols of fruitfulness and multiplication, alternating with golden bells which rang when Aaron was wearing the robe while ministering to the Lord in the Holy of Holies. The bells had the very practical function of making a sound so that the other priests, who were not allowed into the Holy of Holies, would know that the high priest has not died during his service (Exodus 28:35).

The Tunic

The tunic or coat was piece number five, made of fine linen, embroidered, and interwoven with coloured threads (verse 39). The robe was white, to speak of righteousness, as with the ephod. It also reminds us of the robes of righteousness (Isaiah 61:10) which God gives His followers so that He sees the righteousness of His son when they approach the throne of grace with boldness (Hebrews 4:16).

The Turban

The turban was the sixth part of the garments. It was also made of fine linen, symbolizing righteousness and pointed upwards. When Joshua, the high priest, stood before the Lord (Zechariah 3:1), he was given a change of garments and a pure, clean, bright, unadulterated turban (verse 5). After Joshua received his new, pure garments, the angel of the Lord testified to him that the Lord would 'bring forth his servant, the branch' (Verse 8, KJV).

The Gold Plate

The gold plate on the forehead was the penultimate piece of the garments. It was made from pure gold, a symbol of holiness, purity and testing, and placed on blue lace, representing the Holy Spirit. There was an engraving on the plate, *Kodesh YHWH*, meaning 'holy to the Lord.' Jesus' followers are priests (I Peter 2:5 and 9) and have the mark of God on their foreheads (Revelation 9:4). The white turban and the gold plate point towards the helmet of salvation (Ephesians 6:17). The literal meaning of the Greek phrase expressed as helmet describes a movement around the head. How fitting! They also remind us to take every thought captive (II Corinthians 10:5) and to be transformed by renewing our minds to understand the good, pleasant and perfect will of God (Romans 12:2).

The Breeches

The breeches or undergarments are the final part of the garments. They had the very practical function of covering the priests from the hips to the thighs and were worn for decency. What a prophetic meaning the garments of the high priest describe. They speak of holiness, purity, testing, the royalty of Jesus, the Holy Spirit, cleansing, the Covenant, the Passover, forgiveness, salvation, the first and second Adam. They also represent righteousness, consecration to the Lord, the book of life, the New Jerusalem, the helmet of salvation, Jesus as the precious cornerstone, the foundations of Israel and the church. Finally they tell us that Jesus' followers are sealed by God as His priests. Take a deep breath and let these prophetic truths resonate in you.

Marking Physical and Spiritual Space

As my last example, I want to look into art which marks physical and spiritual space in the Old Testament. When God gave the blueprint of the tabernacle to Moses, He spoke of curtains, *yeriyah*, meaning hanging. The tabernacle itself was made with 'ten curtains of fine twisted linen' (Exodus 26:1 and 36:8), with blue, purple, and scarlet threads. We have already seen these materials and colours in the garments of the high priest. These curtains were plaited or woven with cherubim, the same figures as on top of the Ark of the Covenant, symbolizing the presence of God. God also commanded the Israelites to make curtains of goat hair (Exodus 26:7 and 36:14) as a covering, *ohel* for the tabernacle, *mishkan*. The two Hebrew words here can also be translated as 'a tent over the dwelling place.' The curtain at the front of the tabernacle was folded over (Exodus 26:9) to mark the entrance into the dwelling place. Remember that it was made from fine, twisted linen with blue, purple, and scarlet threads and had cherubim, the symbols for the presence of God, embroidered on them. Another curtain was made in the same way and hung in front of the door of the tabernacle (Exodus 26:36), foreshadowing Jesus, who calls himself 'the door' in John 10:9, and who is the only way to enter into God's presence. We enter into fellowship with the Father through the Holy Spirit, symbolised by blue threads. Jesus opened the way by His sacrifice, the red threads, and He makes us kings (Revelation 1:6) as He is the King of Kings, denoted by purple threads.

There is another curtain in the tabernacle. It divides the Holy Place from the Holy of Holies and is described as being made in the same way as the first ones (Exodus 26:31). It carries the same prophetic symbolism, but the word used for it is different, *poreketh*, which is often translated as veil – and not as curtain. It comes from a root word which means to break apart or to fracture.[102] This word puts the focus on the fact that there is a strong separation between two spaces, not that something is just hanging as with *yeriyah*, simply a curtain. In Hebrews 10:19-20, the author of the epistle compares the veil in the temple with Jesus' flesh and says that Jesus made a new way for us through His blood to enter into the Holy of Holies. The word for veil in Greek contains the preposition *katah*. It means against or apart and refers to the same separation of space as the veil in the tabernacle. In Jesus' time, the colours seen in the curtains or veils were called the 'colours of the temple.'[103]

Important keys in Scripture regarding fabric art:

'Moses built an altar and called it The LORD is my Banner' (Exodus 17:15).

'Make a curtain of blue, purple and scarlet yarn and finely twisted linen, with cherubim woven into it by a skilled worker' (Exodus 26:31).

The priestly garments in Exodus 28.

'And Elijah took his *mantle*, and wrapped it together, and smote the waters, and they were divided hither and thither, so that they two went over on dry ground' (II Kings 2:8, KJV).

'In that day the Root of Jesse will stand as a *banner* for the peoples; the nations will rally to him, and his resting place will be glorious' (Isaiah 11:10).

Chapter Eight: Prophetic Music

We might be used to a prophetic word being spoken or written. In our modern times, people often use mobile devices to record words they receive. We can also sing prophecy or express it with instruments and there is a lot of this sort of prophetic expression in Scripture. Let us dive in and see how deep God will take us with prophetic music.

God sings

In Zephaniah 3 there is a part of Scripture entitled in some translations 'Israel's Joy and Restoration.' Verse 17 says that YHWH Elohim will rejoice, spin around in intense emotion over Israel with singing. People have said that sound, music and song, is part of God's being, not something He created. In the same way, creativity is part of God's being, not something He created. God made one being specifically to reflect His beauty, creativity, and sound, Lucifer, who was made extremely beautiful (Ezekiel 28:13-15). His Hebrew name in Isaiah 14:12 is *heylel*, meaning brightness. It comes from the verb *halal* which means to shine in sound and colour, to celebrate, to give light, and to praise.[104] Unfortunately, he did not know how to handle being a mirror of God's beauty, creativity, and sound. Instead, he became proud and was cast out of heaven (Isaiah 14:12). This is one reason why he is now the chief opponent of God and wants to twist, corrupt, destroy worship, beauty, music and art.

When Jesus instituted communion and gave new meaning to the Passover meal, there is a detail that is often overlooked. In Matthew 26:30 and in Mark 14:26, we read that Jesus and the disciples went to the Mount of Olives after they had sung a hymn, ie celebrated God in song. Mark and Matthew clearly tell us that Jesus sang with His disciples. They were all Jews, so the hymn at the Passover meal was most likely a portion of Psalm 113-118 (the 'Hallel'), probably sung antiphonally.

We see the same Greek word for singing in Hebrews 2:12, in the context of verses 5-18 speaking about Jesus. Verse 12 says that He will 'sing praise unto God in the midst of the congregation.' This statement is a direct quotation from Psalm 22:22. The verb for sing or praise in this Psalm is *halal* at which we have already looked. A different word for singing is used in Romans 15:9, *psallo*, which means to sing and 'to play on a stringed instrument.' Romans 15:8-13 is titled 'Christ the Hope of Jews and Gentiles' in some English translations. Verse 9 speaks of the Christ singing unto God's name and professing it among the Gentiles, which is also a quotation from the Psalms. In Psalm 18:49, David sings that he 'will give thanks to YHWH among the Gentiles and sing praises to His name.' The Hebrew term for singing in this passage is *zamar*, which also means to sing and to play on a stringed instrument.

We need to pay attention to the fact that all four instances in which we read of Jesus singing are in a corporate framework. The first one speaks about Jesus singing with His disciples. The passage from Hebrews speaks about Him singing in the congregation, while Romans shows Him praising His Father in music and song among the Gentiles. The reason for this is also stated in that verse: so that 'the Gentiles might glorify God for his mercy' (KJV). There are many references in Scripture to the Spirit singing in us and through us. We will see a lot of them as we continue to look into more aspects of prophetic music.

Prophetic Singing

Paul explains, in Ephesians 5, how we should follow God as His children. After we are exhorted to be continually filled to overflowing with the Holy Spirit (verse 18), He challenges us to 'give utterance' in psalms (set pieces of music accompanied by instruments), hymns (songs of celebration accompanied by music), and spiritual songs.

The last term for song is *ode*, which is a very general and generic term for anything sung. It is a song inspired by the Spirit. There are many examples of songs inspired by the Spirit - prophetic songs - both in the Old and the New Testaments.

Let us first look at five of these examples in the New Testament. The first three relate to Jesus' birth. In Luke 1:46-56, we see a prophetic song by Mary. This passage of Scripture is often called 'the Magnificat' as it describes what God has done for and in her through the incarnation of His son. It prophetically declares God's character. The term translated as said in verse 46, *epo*, does not simply denote that something is spoken, but relates to *phao*, which means to let light shine and to be luminous.[105] It signifies a bright, joyful, luminous declaration. There are at least another five Greek verbs meaning to say[106], none of which have this meaning of shining forth something with joy.

In verses 68-79 of Chapter 1 Luke, John the Baptist's father, Zechariah, sings a prophetic song about the character of God in response to the fact that he and his wife have had a son although she was 'old and barren' (Luke 1:36). This passage of Scripture is often called 'the Benedictus.' When Joseph and Mary presented Jesus at the temple and offered the prescribed sacrifice for the birth of a male Israelite, there was a man named Simeon present. His name comes from a Hebrew root word conveying to hear intelligently or attentively, to understand, and to be obedient.[107] This man was waiting for the Messiah, the 'consolation of Israel' (Luke 2:25, KJV). The Holy Spirit was with him. The Holy Spirit had revealed to Simeon that he would not die until he had seen the Messiah and, on this particular day, led him into the temple. He sings a prophecy over Jesus in verses 28-32 and prophesies about who Jesus is and what he will do. The verb here translated as said in most English translations is the same *epo* that we already encountered in Mary's song above. This passage of Scripture is often called the 'Nunc Dimittis' - 'release now'.

The fourth reference to prophetic singing is in Acts 16:16-40. Paul and Silas have been beaten and thrown into prison. At midnight they pray, worship, and sing hymns (song of celebration) to God. Their songs had several results. First, the earth quakes violently, then the prison doors open, and the chains fall off all the prisoners. The final consequence is that the jailer and his family get saved (verses 25-34). What a result of celebrating God in song!

The last reference is in Philippians 2, where Paul writes, in verses six to eleven, about what Jesus did for us. He became like one of us, humbled Himself and became obedient to death on a cross. The result is that God exalted Him above all. Paul writes that every tongue will confess that Jesus Christ is Lord and every knee will bow before Him. I have heard this passage put to music and sung in worship and I must say it gave me the chills, as the truth proclaimed in song touched me at that moment. This passage is often called the 'hymn of the incarnation.'

Now let us look into six examples from the Old Testament. Two songs are recorded in Exodus 15, one sung by Moses and the other by his sister Miriam. The song of Moses in verses one to nineteen not only describes what God did as the Israelites crossed the Red Sea, verses 1-13, but also gives a spiritual interpretation of the facts, in verses two and six. Furthermore, the song prophesies what will happen to the inhabitants of Pelehsheth, Edom, Moab, and Kenaan. It then speaks of the taking of the Promised Land, verses 16 and 17, and that God will reign forever, verse 18. These last events are all in the future. Right after Moses' song, his sister Miriam, the prophetess, leads the women in circular dances and antiphonal singing, repeating what her brother had started. We see this in verses 20 and 21. This is not just a prophetic song, but also a prophetic dance.

The entire chapter of Judges 5 is a prophetic song by Deborah and Barak. Deborah was a prophetess (Judges 4:4), the wife of Lapidoth, meaning multiple lights. Her name comes from the root verb *dabar*, which means to speak, but also to command and to declare.[108] Barak's name means lightning or a flashing sword.[109] These two people led the armies to free Israel from the Canaanites and now they sing a song of victory. Again, the song does not only describe the facts but gives spiritual interpretations. In verse 23, this song speaks of curses and in verse 24 of blessings. The last verse of the song prophesies about the enemies of the Lord perishing (curses) and those who love Him being as the sun (blessings).

David sang a song of deliverance. It is recorded in chapter 22 of II Samuel. David gives spiritual visions and interpretations of what God has done. Verse 4 recites 'I will call upon the Lord, who is worthy to be praised' and verse 47 says 'The Lord liveth, and blessed be the rock, and let the God of my salvation be exalted.' These are verses found in *Michael O'Shields'* work entitled 'I will call upon the Lord.' David describes the character of God in verses 26 to 28 and verse 31. In verses 44 to 46 he prophesies about the future of his kingdom and reign. You might be aware that II Samuel 22 is nearly identical to Psalm 18. There are only a few words which are different. The fact that this song is recorded twice in the Old Testament shows us how important its message is.

Miriam's song was corporate as she led the women and Deborah's and Barak's song was a duet. We see another corporate prophetic song in II Chronicles 20:1-26. King Jehoshaphat of Judah fights against the armies of Ammon and Moab. In verses 15 to 17, God gives the people a prophecy about how His victory will come about. They then praise God for this in a loud voice in verse 19 and as they go into battle, they appoint singers, verse 21, who will 'praise the beauty of holiness.' They go out in front of the army and sing, 'Praise the Lord, for his mercy [steadfast love, kindness, beauty, favour] endures forever.' They prophesy about the character of God and that He will not change in the future. We see in the following verse how God destroys the enemy armies. In verse 26, the people thank God and bless Him. The Hebrew word for bless is *barak*. Do you see the connection to Judges 5? The place where they thank God is called the Valley of Berachah, which comes from *barak* and means blessing also. There are three different verbs used for praise in verses 21 and 22. *Halal*, which also means to shine, to boast, and to celebrate. *Yadah*, which conveys the extension of one's hands in worship, and *tehillah*, which is related to *halal*, but bears the significance of spontaneity. *Tehillah* is the verb used in Isaiah 42:10 and 12 to praise the Lord in a new song.

The last reference for prophetic song in the Old Testament comes from the prophet Isaiah in chapter 42. This chapter of Isaiah is a far-reaching prophecy which speaks about God's plan to redeem the nations. The chapter is divided into three parts. The first part is verses one to nine in which God speaks about His chosen servant, ie Jesus. This passage contains detailed descriptions of Jesus' first coming. Then, in verses 10 to 12, He commands the nations to sing a new song, a prophetic song to the Lord in response to His prophecy about who Jesus is and what He will do. In this sense, you can call Isaiah 42 an instructive prophecy. This singing is not the singing of regular or known songs, but is a singing that requires prophetic instruction. He wants it to be shouted from the mountaintops. The ends of the earth shall sing. The coastlands shall sing; the islands shall sing; the wilderness shall sing; the cities shall sing; the villages shall sing; the high places shall sing. The last part, verses 13 to 17, speaks about God giving His judgement to the nations.

There are numerous other prophetic songs in the Old Testament. You can find some in Numbers 21:47, I Samuel 10:5, Isaiah 5:1-7, Isaiah 12, Isaiah 26, Isaiah 27, Isaiah 51:11, Isaiah 52:8-9, and Habakkuk 3:17-19 to name a few. And do not forget that God 'inhabits the praises of his people' (Psalm 22:3).

We heard a story of a prophetic song being written in 2018 at Bethel Church in Redding, California. The son of a couple affiliated with the church was airlifted to hospital a few days before Christmas. The parents called upon people to pray for him. People in the church called the intercession for this boy 'a symphony of prayer.'[110] A few weeks later, the parents sent word that the doctors had said that the boy might not survive the night. One of the worship leaders decided to confront the 'giant of unbelief' he faced as he was interceding. He says that a song[111] started coming out in the face of the giant:

I raise a Hallelujah in the presence of my enemy
I raise a Hallelujah louder than the unbelief
I raise Hallelujah my weapon is a melody.[112]

This is part of the stanza of the song. Their community began to sing this song as one note in the symphony of prayer. The boy was healed and the community still raises a Hallelujah and sings this prophetic song to glorify God. They say that when you sing, prison walls come falling down and heaven invades earth (Matthew 6:10).

The New Song

What, then, is new song? We see this phrase, *chadash shiyr*, in many places.[113] In the New Testament, we see the corresponding Greek phrase, *kainos ode*, in Revelation 5:9 and 14:3. *Chadash* describes a newness that is fresh or spontaneous.[114] *Shiyr* focusses on the process of singing, not so much the (written down) song. The new song is a spontaneous song under the inspiration of the Holy Spirit. Psalm 40:3 says that God put this song into the singer's mouth. I cannot tell you why, at a certain time or in a certain meeting, God choses to give a message by singing through someone, and why at other times He does not.

The new song can be a singer's song *to* the Lord. In that case, it is often a song of praise and acclamation (Psalm 40:3 and Psalm 149:1). But it can also be a song *from* the Lord to the people (as in Zephaniah 3:17). In that case it is a prophetic song - a *rhema* word of the Lord. Of course, it is not a term for the word from God, as is Scripture. However, a song from God communicates His heart at a certain time in a certain situation. He gave one prophetic song to a group of intercessors during a worship and intercession time at one of the high points in the nation of Cyprus, in May 2019. A group of us had spent time singing, interceding, and prophesying over the nation. This is the spontaneous song we received that morning:

I desire your heart.
I desire your thoughts.
I desire you.
I desire your fields of emotions,
I desire your mind.

Come to me as I call.
Come to me as I call.

O bride, give your all to me as I call.

When we sing a new song, we sing what God puts into our mouth. It is Christ in us, the hope of glory (Colossians 1:27) singing through us. It is he river of God's Spirit and His living water pouring out from us (John 7:38) in song. We become ambassadors of His message to individuals, congregations, cities and nations. As it is prophetic, it points to Jesus (Revelation 19:10) and encourages, exhorts and comforts (I Corinthians 14:3). The new song can be sung by an individual or by a group of people in perfect unity. In Isaiah 42:10, groups of people are commanded to sing the new song. In Revelation 5:9, the four beasts and the 24 elders sing in unity and, in Revelation 14:3, 144,000 people sing the new song in unity.

It is interesting to see what Matt Redman said at a worship leaders' conference[115] about prophetic singing:

Praying or singing prophetically is like walking a tight rope; sometimes all I have is a line in my head and I think "OK then, here we go." The thing about walking a tight rope is that you mustn't look down. In the same way when stepping out in the prophetic keep looking "straight ahead" towards God. Keep focusing on the Lord, focusing towards Jesus.

As we sing what God puts into us, we focus on Him. You can follow a few simple guidelines when you walk this tight rope. Focus on what God is saying. You do not need to add anything. If it is a short song - fine. There is no need to stretch it into many verses. Listen carefully to the voice of the Spirit. He flows in music as He did in the Tabernacle of David. More on that later.

Be aware of your own authority. What is God showing you? As you are obedient to singing the message He is giving you, God will probably give you more authority to deliver His words in this way in the future. Be in step with Him. Follow the current flow of the river. Don't change the musical flow or rhythm or the direction of the meeting. Become part of the message. Identify with what you are singing about. See if you need to react to the message or if the people in the meeting or situation in which you are singing need to take action. Check with the facilitators of the meeting in which you are singing. If you sing over an individual, check with your own spiritual leaders as you would in any other case of prayer or prophecy. The general guidelines outlined earlier apply.

The Tabernacle of David

The worship in the Tabernacle of David is a milestone in the expression of prophetic worship in the Old Testament. Many things have been written both about the Tabernacle and the type of worship in David's tabernacle. I will point to basic insights as they pertain to prophetic music.

During the reign of King David (c. 1000 BC to c. 960 BC), two tabernacles existed - the Tabernacle of Moses at Gibeon (I Chronicles 21:29)[116] and the Tabernacle of David at the City of David (I Chronicles 15:1). Although the Tabernacle of Moses still existed, the Ark of the Covenant was not in it any more. When the Philistines captured the Ark (I Samuel 4:1-11) the presence of the Lord left Moses' tabernacle. Israel became *ichabod,* meaning without glory. The Philistines sent the Ark back (I Samuel 6), but then it stayed in Bethshemesh, in Kirjathjearim (I Samuel 7), which is only five miles from Gibeon and eight miles from Jerusalem. The Ark was not, however, put back into Moses' Tabernacle.

Almost ten years into David's kingship (c. 990 BC), he brought the Ark to Jerusalem after having consulted with all his leaders (I Chronicles 13:1) and all of Israel assembled together (verses 2-4). They all agreed that it was the Lord's will to bring the Ark back. David stated that Israel did not 'enquire' at it during the days of Saul (verse 3). The Hebrew word for enquire, *darash,* can also mean to worship.[117] But he did not put the Ark back into the Tabernacle of Moses. Instead he pitched a tent for it in the City of David, and there the presence of the Lord returned (I Chronicles 16:33 and 17:5).

Some people argue that Moses' tabernacle was only for the time when the Israelites were wandering in the desert. It was actually built as a portable tent (Exodus 40). David's tent was not meant to be moved, the argument goes, but stayed in one place until Solomon built the first temple. When God made His covenant with David, He said that He would appoint a place for Israel that they will 'move no more' (II Samuel 7:10, KJV).

The amazing thing about David's tent is that God did allow open access to the Ark and did not apply His own law to it. In Deuteronomy 12:1-28, God declares that there is one place of worship He will choose and any other place is forbidden. David departed from this law, but still the presence of the Lord returned. Scripture does not give an explanation. Not only was there no separation between the people and the Ark in David's tabernacle, David also instituted prophetic worship and prophetic music before the Ark, in the presence of the Lord.

The Law of Moses did not speak about music in the tabernacle. The only musical sound in the tabernacle was the blowing of trumpets at the appointed celebrations and at the beginning of each month (Numbers 10:10). In the time of Hezekiah, we are reminded that Nathan the prophet and Gad the seer commanded David to add music to the worship (II Chronicles 29:25). We see the significant difference in the types of worship in the two tabernacles described in Hebrews 12:18-24. The Mosaic way of engaging with the Lord is described in verses 18 to 21 in which the people are terrified and cannot bear to even hear the voice of the Lord. Even Moses is full of fear. The Davidic way of engaging with the Lord - foreshadowing the New Covenant - is described in verses 22 to 24. It is represented as a picture of the heavenly Jerusalem, which is described as the tabernacle of God (Revelation 21:3) where God's glory dwells (Revelation 21:23). Those who are saved walk in its light (Revelation 21:24).

David was also a musician and had ample experience with prophetic music. He had learned to worship the Lord in music and song while tending his father's sheep. When an evil spirit repeatedly plagued King Saul, he sent for David to skilfully play the harp and the evil spirit left Saul (I Samuel 16:16-23). David wrote many psalms which were a by-product of his worship. He is called the 'sweet psalmist of Israel' in II Samuel 23:1. It does not come as a surprise that he would chose music and song to express worship before the Ark in a new way. The worship in the tent of David has been called New Covenant worship in the Old Covenant. This is because God wants to be worshiped on earth as He is in heaven (Matthew 6:10, Revelation 4 and 5).

What, then, characterized this Davidic worship? Much has been written on this topic. Again, I will focus on basic keys. This type of worship included musical instruments, singing, chanting, standing, bowing, lifting hands, clapping, dancing and processions. It was often prophetic (I Chronicles 25:1) and new songs, both prophetic and spontaneous, were sung (Psalm 33:3, 96:1, and 149:1). It focussed on God's beauty, character and deeds. Some of the worship was structured (I Chronicles 25:6) and some was improvised (25:1). The singers and those playing the instruments were priests who had been trained for this type of service. We see this when we look into I Chronicles 25:6 and 25:8 which speak of direction and the cooperation of teachers and students. We understand today that, as musicians and singers, we need to develop our skills so that we can use them naturally when the Spirit asks us to flow with Him.

The sheer number of singers and musicians involved is also impressive. In I Chronicles 25:4-10, we see 862 being called from the children of Aaron and the Levites. The number of the musicians praising the Lord grew to 4,000 (I Chronicles 25:5). This was not a few musicians getting together to have a session now and again, but was an organized orchestra and choir that rivalled modern music productions. In Psalm 68:24-25, David states that even God Himself joined in the processions. It might be worthy to note that young women[118] were in the procession with tambourines. The singers also danced circle dances in the sanctuary (Psalm 149:3 and 150:4). Imagine your own church dancing in a circle dance and prophesying to music during your Sunday morning service!

Another important element of this worship was that it went on day and night, without interruption (I Chronicles 9:33). Ongoing, uninterrupted worship is not a modern thing. Remember the monks of Bangor Abbey who sustained worship and prayer for 250 years (558 AD – 810 AD) or the Moravians who sustained it for over 100 years. God's spirit enables these things to occur and even calls people today into such service! The singers and musicians were chosen for a 'service' (I Chronicles 25:1), translated from *abodah*. This word does not talk about a liturgy or a structured church service. It comes from a root word, *abad*, which means that someone is in bondage.[119] The singers and musicians are called to be servants. They serve God as they sing and prophesy to music. During this prophetic worship, God's presence would become manifest. We are told that God 'inhabits the praise of his people' (Psalm 22:3). In Psalm 67:1 and 80:7 we read that God makes His face shine upon the people in the sanctuary as they worship Him.

What enabled David to establish such prophetic worship? David had a quality which we all need as we are involved in creating prophetically, whether in song, music, painting, sculpture, writing, design or any other creative expression. He was a man after God's own heart (Acts 13:22). This means that he chose again and again, in all circumstances of life, to turn toward God. His soul 'thirsts for God' (Psalm 42:2) and he 'strengthens himself in the Lord' (I Samuel 30:6). The verb translated strengthen is *chazaq* in the Hebrew. The essential meaning of this verb is to seize.[120] David seizes God when he is extremely distressed and his own people want to stone him. Do you seize God in challenging situations? Do you 'gaze upon his beauty all the days of your life' (Psalm 27:4)?

This attitude of heart is what would lead David to swear seven times as a symbol of completeness and to vow[121] that he will not go home and sleep until he finds and establishes a habitation, a dwelling place for God (Psalm 132:5). This vow was fulfilled ten years into his kingship when he brought the Ark into the City of David in Jerusalem. The fulfilment of this vow was the beginning of the foreshadowing of prophetic worship, which is ultimately fulfilled in the heavenly realms in front of God's throne (Revelation 4 and 5). It is interesting to realize that David makes note of 'Ephrathah,' ie Bethlehem, in Psalm 132. He says that they have heard of the place of the Lord at Ephrathah. Bethlehem was both his and Jesus' birthplace. As he makes the vow which brings the foreshadowing of the worship around God's throne in heaven to the earth and he connects it with the first coming of the Messiah. We do not take prophetic worship lightly. The spirit of prophecy is the testimony of Jesus.

This testimony was also prophesied by Asaph, a prophet, singer, composer and musician. He and his sons were among those chosen by David and the leaders of his army to prophesy with instruments in the Tabernacle (I Chronicles 25:1-2). Asaph wrote 12 Psalms, involving Psalm 50 and Psalms 73 to 83. He prophesies in Psalm 78:1-4, that the coming Messiah will speak in parables. Matthew quotes this passage from Psalm 78 and calls Asaph a prophet when he explains that Jesus spoke in parables (Matthew 13:34-35). Isn't that astonishing? The family of Asaph, the sons of Asaph, are mentioned centuries later when leaders in Israel re-establish Davidic worship. This happened under King Joash[122] (843BC to 797 BC), King Hezekiah[123] (c. 739 BC to c. 687 BC), King Josiah[124] (c. 648 BC to c. 609 BC), Zerubbabel[125] (mentioned c. 538 BC to c. 520 BC), and Nehemiah[126] (mentioned c. 445 BC to c. 432 BC).

Both the Old and the New Testaments also speak about Davidic worship being lifted up again in the future. The prophet Amos talked about it in the last verses of his book (9:11-12):

In that day "I will restore David's fallen shelter – I will repair its broken walls and restore its ruins – and will rebuild it as it used to be, so that they may possess the renant of Edom and all the nations that bear my name," declares the Lord, who will do these things.

At the Council of Jerusalem in Acts 15:15-17 James quoted this passage from Amos. The Council had been called to talk about sharing the gospel with the Gentiles and the question whether Gentile believers needed to be circumcised in order to keep the Law of Moses. Peter, Paul, Barnabas, and James all came to the conclusion that Gentile believers did not have to be circumcised to keep the Law of Moses, but only should abstain from fornication, from meat offered to idols, and from blood and meat from strangled animals (verses 20 and 29). The apostles and elders were very clear about the fact that the time in which the Gentiles will come into the Kingdom of God had started.

James supports this fact with the passage from Amos which, in verse 12, states that Israel shall inherit the remnant of the Gentiles who are 'called by [the Lord's] name.' The fact that Israel will inherit or possess Gentiles refers to the fact that God will graft Gentile branches into the original Olive Tree (Romans 11:17-24). The word for remnant comes from the root word *leipo* which means to leave.[127] Those Gentiles that will be grafted in are those who leave the kingdom of darkness and enter into the Kingdom of Light (Colossians 1:13, Acts 26:18).

This process has happened throughout the centuries since Jesus' resurrection. Many people have written about the meaning of the restoration of the tabernacle of David. There are many other aspects one can talk about. I will focus only on one further aspect which is the restoration of prophetic worship. Not every movement of the Gentiles coming into the Kingdom during the centuries also featured a restoration of prophetic worship. 'The hallmark of every revival [in history] is the new music birthed.'[128] It was birthed in Spirit-led spontaneous worship, singing, testimony and ministry. We can look, for example, at the songs written during the reformation in Germany; the songs the Wesleys wrote; the Salvation Army songs; the songs of the Great Awakening; and, the revival in Azuza Street. We could also include3 the songs from the Jesus Movement and many others. If we only consider the Welsh Revival of 1904-1905, we will understand that before the revival started, Wales had already become known as the 'Land of Song.' The revival songs written in the next few years signified this revival's specific emphasis on the move of God sweeping through the land. So it was with every revival that specific songs were birthed, some of which we still sing today.

Psalms – Poems Set to Notes

Many psalms were written by David, and by Asaph, and some composed by other authors. Many were a by-product of worship. They let us look into the whole range of human emotion. When we look into the Psalms of David,[129] we see that he often reflects on his own lack of perfection. At the same time, he makes a choice to turn to the Lord in his distress and to praise him in all circumstances. We can see a conversation ensuing between David and God which often become prophetic. The Psalms have been called 'songs of the heart.'[130] There are many ways to divide the book of Psalms into subsections. I will not go into details here, but only show a few basic ones.

There are the 'Psalms of Asaph,' numbers 50 and 73 to 83. There is the '*Hallel,*' Psalm 113 to 118, chanted at various Jewish festivals. There are the 'songs of ascent,' Psalm 120-134. One explanation for them being called ascent is that the Jews would sing these songs as they ascended to Jerusalem to visit the temple for three annual festivals. Jerusalem lies on several hills and the temple was on a hill in Jerusalem. One can also divide the Psalms according to their themes, ie lament, thanksgiving, praise, trust, wisdom, etc.

The Israelites sang the Psalms. We do not know the actual vocalization and exact pronunciation of the Hebrew in which the Psalms were written, but the Hebrew word translated 'Psalm' is *mizmor*. It appears 57 times, only in the book of Psalms, and means a poem set to notes. *Mizmor*'s root word means to touch the strings of an instrument or to make music accompanied by the voice.[131] If we want to understand more about how the Psalms were sung, we need to look at the structure of the poems. The most significant structural characteristic of the Psalms is the internal parallelism. It can be seen in several different forms:[132]

Synonymic – two half-verses contain the same thought while one half-verse responds to the other.

Antithetic – a thought is carried in two half-verses opposing each other.

Synthetic – the second of two half-verses completes the statement of the first.

Climactic – a thought is built upon from line to line ending in a culmination.

This parallel structure of the Psalms was reflected in the ways the Levites, who were professional musicians, sang them: antiphonally, in two alternating choirs, and in responses, a soloist alternating with a single choir. There are some headings left in the text which show us that there used to be instructions regarding their musical presentation. One of them is 'for the choir director.' There are possible tunes mentioned in Psalm 6, 9, 12, 22, 53, and 56-59 as well as possible instruments in Psalm 4-6, 8, 54-55, 60-61, and 69. The interpretations of all these words used for tunes and instruments are the subject of intense debate among Biblical and musical scholars.

The Psalms are one major building block of Hebrew liturgies. Complete Psalms as well as phrases and sections of Psalms have found their way into the Jewish prayerbook. No other Biblical book holds the same prominence in the liturgies. We will see more about the Psalms as prophetic literature in the chapter on writing.

Music Therapy

There is another purpose of music which is very close to prophecy through music, which is music therapy. It is defined as 'the professional use of music and its elements as an intervention in medical, educational, and everyday environments with individuals, groups, families, or communities who seek to optimize their quality of life and improve their physical, social, communicative, emotional, intellectual, and spiritual health and wellbeing.'[133] Let us look into this definition and see how it relates to prophetic music.

When God speaks through music, He is very *professional*. He is the ultimate professional (Genesis 1:1), not only in questions of music. When God speaks through music, He *intervenes* in the earthly realm with truth from the heavenly realm (Matthew 6:10). God can heal through music. He changes our *medical* state (I Samuel 16:14-23); He changes our *educational* understanding as we prophesy through music (I Samuel 10:5), and He breaks into our *everyday* environment through His prophetic music (Judges 5). God speaks through music to *individuals* (II Kings 3:15) as well as entire *communities* (II Chronicles 20:17-23). We seek to optimize our quality of life as we seek the life which Jesus promised in abundance (John 10:10). God's original plan for mankind was physical, emotional, mental, and spiritual health.

I would like to relate these phenomena to an incident in the Old Testament. In I Samuel 16:14-23, an evil spirit torments King Saul.

He asks for a skilled harp player to come and to bring him relief. David comes to play before Saul and as he plays, the evil spirit leaves him. There is a connection between David's playing and Saul's deliverance. The deliverance Saul experiences was based upon the playing of David.

When we see the details, we find that David's playing brings deliverance to Saul in two ways; both spiritual deliverance and physical deliverance. Saul experienced spiritual deliverance because the spirit departed or withdrew from him, as a result of the music. This is not something passive that happened, the spirit actively withdrew. Saul also was refreshed or revived physically. The verb in the Hebrew translated refreshed is related to *ruach*, meaning to blow.[134] It describes what the Spirit of God, the *ruach*, does. We see that even the physical deliverance of Saul is tied back into the underlying spiritual reality. Aluede and Ekewenu[135] call the spiritual deliverance 'psycholytic musical therapy' and the physical deliverance 'algolytic musical therapy.' Music therapy is used in cases of mental health needs, developmental and learning disabilities, aging related conditions, substance abuse, brain injuries and pain relief. It has shown quantifiable benefits in cases of trauma counseling, crisis intervention, disaster response and relief efforts. God is still YHWH Rapha (Exodus 15:26), the Lord who heals. He still speaks through music and song into our lives. He still sings over us and changes spiritual and physical realities.

Important keys in Scripture regarding music:

'Whenever the spirit from God came on Saul, David would take up his lyre and play. Then relief would come to Saul; he would feel better, and the evil spirit would leave him' (I Samuel 16:23).

David's song of praise in II Samuel 22.

'David, together with the commanders of the army, set apart some of the sons of Asaph, Heman and Jeduthun for the ministry of prophesying, accompanied by harps, lyres and cymbals' (I Chronicles 25:1).

'He put a new song in my mouth, a hymn of praise to our God. Many will see and fear the LORD and put their trust in him' (Psalm 40:3).

'The LORD your God is with you, the Mighty Warrior who saves. He will take great delight in you; in his love he will no longer rebuke you, but will rejoice over you with *singing*' (Zephaniah 3:17).

'When they [Jesus and the disciples] had sung a hymn, they went out to the Mount of Olives' (Matthew 26:30 and Mark 14:26).

And they sang a new song, saying: "You are worthy to take the scroll and to open its seals, because you were slain, and with your blood you purchased for God persons from every tribe and language and people and nation (Revelation 5:9).

Chapter Nine: Painting, Carving, and Engraving

Colours

When we look at these three techniques, we first of all need to gain a basic understanding about how the ancient Israelites saw colours. In the Old Testament the term for colour is *ayin*, meaning outward appearance. When thinking about colour, you might remember Joseph's coat of many colours, which we read about in Genesis 37:3. The term applied here, however, is not *ayin* but *pas*.[136] A translation closer to the original meaning of the word would probably be of many breadth or of many threads. The Israelites did not have a specific verb expressing to colour or to paint. They used *chaqah*, but its meaning leans more towards carving and delineating.[137]

The Israelites also did not develop a clearly distinguished language for colours. This is very typical for the Orient or Middle East ancient people groups. The Hebrews did not describe people or things according to their outward appearance, but according to their inward character. This means that even words which are translated as colours often describe the inward reality and not the actual colour. There are actually only three words which were used distinctly for colours; blue, red, and white.

Blue: *tekeleth* is a word for the mussel which was used to produce the respective colour or dye.[138] You find this word in the descriptions of the high priest's garments as well as the curtains and fabrics in the tabernacle (Exodus 25 and Numbers 4:6 and 15:38). It is one of the three colours mentioned repeatedly for the tabernacle ('blue, and purple, and scarlet') and is used 49 times in the Old Testament. We see a related word, *shecheleth,* in the mixture for the frankincense in the tabernacle (Exodus 30:34). It is a spice, apparently made from the same mussel. We can notice that even in this distinctive word, the Hebrews did not describe the actual colour but used the name for the animal from which it came.

Red: There are six main words which express the colour red:

Karmiyl, which is a brilliant crimson. The word is probably not of Hebrew origin and depicts the dye obtained from a bug.[139] It is used in II Chronicles 2:7, 2:14, and 3:14. You can guess that the English word 'carmine' is related to it.

Shaniy, often rendered as 'scarlet,' is the name of the insect from which this dye was made.[140] It is used 42 times in the Old Testament. Expensive garments are called scarlet, as in Jeremiah 4:30. It is also used in cleansing ceremonies, as in Numbers 19:6, and that was the colour of the thread which Rahab hung out of her window in Jericho (Joshua 2:18).

Adom, used 7 times in the Old Testament, speaks of blood and its colour. It is related to *adam*, a verb meaning to show blood, which is used ten times in the Old Testament, and related to *admoniy* - used three times in Genesis 25:25, I Samuel 16:12, and 17:42. Although it is a distinct word for colour, it denotes the colour of blood.[141] In II Kings 3:22 water is described as red as blood. Blood is the Hebrew word *dam* which is also related.

Argevan, which speaks of a bluish red and is used only in the book of Daniel 5:7, 16, and 29.[142] Expensive clothing denotes the wearer's high status and is called scarlet or purple.

Tola, which is a maggot and refers to the dye made from it.[143] We find it 43 times in the Old Testament. Seven times it is actually translated as worm.[144] Some translations render it as purple instead of scarlet. This is the third colour mentioned repeatedly for the tabernacle (blue, and purple, and scarlet).

Shashar is translated 'vermillion' in Jeremiah 22:14 and Ezekiel 23:14. It is a red ochre used to paint. The term come from a root which means bright or shrill.[145] We can conclude that this colour was very intense and piercing. Have you ever painted with bright, intense colours? Have you ever worn intense colours? The Israelites used them for the outside of their houses.

There are other words which are rendered as a variety of red, but these do not speak of colours but of being dark or glowing, *chakliyl*, as in Genesis 49:12, fermenting or glowing, *chamar*, as in Psalm 75:8, or of glistening marble or alabaster, *bahat* as in Esther 1:6.

White: The definite word used for white is *laban*.[146] It speaks of the material that bricks were made of and actually looked white. There are 24 passages in the Old Testament containing this word. It is, for instance, applied as a symbol of purity, as in Daniel 12:10. Other words translated white literally mean bleached or dazzling.

Other words for colour are not as clear as blue, red, and white. Black is translated from eight different words and green is translated from at least five different words. Green speaks of vegetation, herbs, freshness, and flourishing things. In Esther 1:6, the term *karpas* actually means 'byssus,' which we read in chapter 7. Purple, *argaman*, is the third colour of the tabernacle along with blue and scarlet. It varied greatly, andhence it is not classified as a distinct colour, according to the kind of shellfish it came from and the different methods of dying fabric. We find the term 38 times in the Old Testament. It speaks of royal or expensive garments and the people who work with this type of dye. Brown is *chum*, which is mentioned four times in Genesis 30 to describe the flocks of Laban and Joseph. Yellow is *tsahob*, mentioned three times in Leviticus 13 to describe hair. In Psalm 68:13, the term translated as yellow is *yeraqraq*.

There are five Hebrew words translated as **gold** which include:

Zahab, which means shimmering. It always describes the actual metal and not just a colour. Even when we read in Exodus 28 and 39 that the ephod was made of gold, blue, purple, and scarlet [yarn], together with finely twisted linen, the gold did not depict just the colour. The Talmud argues that each of the textures was combined in six threads with a seventh of gold leaf, making 28 threads to the texture in total. Sometimes, *zahab* is used metaphorically, as in Job 23:10, but even then it speaks of the metal, and not the colour.

Charuts, which originally meant 'incised', appears it 17 times in the Old Testament and it does not describe the actual metal. It is translated closer to its original meaning as sharp, diligent, threshing instrument, and even as decision.[147] Only one time, in Psalm 68:13, is it used in combination with yellow and it is not clear if *charuts* even describes gold here, although it is often translated that way.

Kethem, describes something 'carved out' like ore. We find it nine times in the Old Testament and none of the passages talk about the colour.

Paz is a word which depicts the gold possibly found in rivers. This means that it was not mined and, thus, not mingled with other metals, but remained pure. None of the nine passages in the Old Testament focus on the colour gold.

Dehab is used 23 times in Ezra and Daniel. It has a similar meaning as *zahab*.

In summary, we see that none of these words focus on the colour gold.

Silver is the Hebrew word *keseph*. Its root word means pale.[148] We find it in 343 verses in the Old Testament. Two related words, *kesiyth* and *kesaph*, both seem to describe silver money. Again, not a single time is something described as having a silver colour without being the metal, silver.

In the New Testament, blue, brown and yellow are not mentioned. The term red, *kokkinos*, is related to the origin of the respective colour, scarlet red. It describes the shape of the insect from which this colour was made.[149] The term appears six times in the New Testament, including Matthew 27:28, where the soldiers put a scarlet robe on Jesus. This shows again that it is difficult to identify colours distinctively in the Bible. In some passages where the term red appears, the Greek words come from the root *pur*, meaning fire.[150] In Matthew 16:2 and 3, the sky is described as like fire or red. In Revelation 6:4 a horse is described as like fire or red and in Revelation 12:3, a dragon is described in the same way. Revelation 19:12 compares Jesus' eyes with fire.

White is translated from the Greek word *leukos* which comes from a root meaning light.[151] We find it in 23 passages of the New Testament. The word describes the colour white in Revelation 1:14 where Jesus' head and hair are likened to bleached wool and snow. The horse in Revelation 19:11 and 14 is also called white. The linen in verse 19:14 is called white and clean. It depicts purity. In Revelation 15:6 and 19:8, *lampros* is often rendered as white, but actually means radiant.

Black is the Greek word *melas*, only used three times to describe hair in Matthew 5:36 and Revelation 6:12, and to describe a horse in Revelation 6:5. Green means *chloros*, which is only used four times to describe green vegetation in Mark 6:39, Revelation 8:9, and 9:4 and to describe a horse, albeit rendered as pale, in Revelation 6:8. Purple is the Greek term *porphura* or its adjective *porphurous*, and is used eight times, always to describe fabric or merchandise. It is the term for the mussel which was used to obtain this dye. Again, even the Greek word focuses on the inner reality, and not the outer colour.

Gold is not mentioned only as a colour in the New Testament. When it is an adjective, *chruseos*, it shows something which is made from actual gold. We see this 16 times in the New Testament. The related word *chrusion* is used nine times, also referring to something made from gold. There are an additional 12 passages which speak about the actual metal, as in Matthew 2:11, where the three wise men give gold to Jesus. Silver is also not mentioned only as a colour. We find silver as a metal, *arguros*, appears four times and something made from silver is mentioned 23 times. You can find the prophetic meaning of colours in Appendix 2

Paint with Anointing

Many times I have heard that the Bible does not mention painting. This has to do with the fact that the Israelites were slaves in Egypt; then nomads on their way to the Promised Land; and, then warriors taking that land over. It was also a result of the second commandment that God gave them not to make graven images or to represent anything in heaven, on earth, or under the earth for the purpose of idolatry. I will deal with this commandment in the next subheading. It is interesting, however, to look at the three areas God forbade them to represent for the purpose of idolatry. They correspond to Philippians 2:10: 'At the name of Jesus every knee shall bow in heaven, on earth and under the earth.' This type of framework does not lend itself to developing a strong painting tradition.

If you do a word search for painting in Scripture, very little is found. The term *sum* or *siym*, which has the general meaning of 'to put', is used 546 times in the Old Testament. One time it is translated as paint in the KJV, in II Kings 9:30, where Jezebel 'paints her face,' ie she puts on make up to look young in order to seduce Jehu as he comes to actually execute her. When we paint prophetically, we do not put make up on to deceive or to cover something. We actually do the opposite and intend to reveal a message from the Lord. We reveal how things truly are in the spiritual and physical realm.

The other term implored to describe paint is *mashach*. We see it in 67 verses in the Old Testament. Its root meaning is to rub.[152] Sixty-six times it is translated as to anoint! We see the command to anoint Aaron and his sons (Exodus 28:41) or to anoint the tabernacle (30:26), which are just two examples. Jeremiah 22:14 is the only place where the English version uses paint. In this passage, the prophet warns Shallum, son of King Josiah of Judah, not to build his house on injustice. This house is described as being rubbed or painted with red ochre or vermillion (KJV). I am not going to build a theology on this one use of the word *mashach*. I want to challenge you as painters, however, to keep in mind when you paint that the term for this process in the Old Testament is the same one which means to anoint or to consecrate! The next time you rub paint or paste on a canvas, wood, glass or any other surface you use, keep in mind that the process you are engaging in is the same process as the anointing of the priests, the tabernacle, the altars etc. in the tabernacle of Moses. Consecrate yourselves as you paint and paint with anointing.

One year after I started to paint prophetically a friend of ours in Germany, Ute Horn, went through a life-threatening illness and had an operation. She survived the operation and went into rehabilitation, not knowing whether or not the operation had caused any permanent harm. During this time, I was inspired to paint something for her. I was still very reluctant to paint for others and quite insecure in this newfound gift. I painted a blue waterfall coming down over several levels, and surrounded by purple structures. I wrote an explanation for the painting, wrapped it, and sent it to Ute while she was at the rehabilitation clinic. This is what she wrote about it in her book concerning her illness:

> One sentence [of the explanation] especially speaks to me: "His water of life will flow through you." Is that not another confirmation for the messages of [other friends], who said that I will bring more fruit to the glory of God? The painting reflects my deeply rooted desire that people will experience the love of God through me and that I can be a channel for this Him.[153]

The painting and a letter from another friend challenged her again to realize that her identity is founded in the Lord and depends on Him, and not on her abilities, her health or her value in society.

Prophetic painting does not only speak to individuals. It is interesting to note that the church throughout the centuries has made art available to explain Biblical truths and to further knowledge of the gospel. One reason for this was that many people could neither read nor write and the clergy believed that the populace did not need to have access to the Bible. Another reason, more important to our cause, is the ability of art to function 'as a mode of reflection on and embodiment of Christian ideas and values and, hence, as constituting a form of theology.'[154] People encounter art with a different part of themselves. Art bypasses the mind and goes directly to the heart. This is where we connect with it and try to make understanding possible.

Pope Benedict XVI addressed these facts during his meeting with artists in the Sistine Chapel on 21 November, 2009. He said that 'Christianity from its earliest days has recognized the value of the arts and has made wise use of their varied language to express her unvarying message of salvation.'[155] Pope John Paul II stressed in his *Letter to*

Artists ten years earlier that both artists and the church are 'passionately dedicated to the search for new "epiphanies" of beauty.'[156] It surprised me that as early as 1964, Pope Paul VI delivered a speech in the Sistine Chapel that told artists that 'your task, your mission, and your art consists in grasping treasures from the heavenly realm of the Spirit and clothing them in words, colours, forms – making them accessible.'[157]

On June 28th 2005, Benedict XVI officially issued a new Compendium of the Catechism of the Catholic Church. This Compendium contains fourteen masterpieces of painting. They are not seen as illustrations but as 'a structural part of the Christian faith.'[158] The Pope understood images as a preaching of the Gospel. He declared that 'today more than ever, in a culture of images, a sacred image can express much more than what can be said in words, and be an extremely effective and dynamic way of communicating the Gospel message.'[159]

At the beginning of Advent that year, a new Liturgical Lectionary went into use in the Catholic Church. It contains 87 images by thirty contemporary Italian artists who all painted in a more or less abstract style. The style of the paintings and the question whether abstract art is not too limited to convey Christian realities led to an intense discussion among Catholic scholars and clergy. Timothy Verdon, at the time a professor at Princeton University and director of the diocesan office for catechesis through art in Florence, argued that 'the use of solely contemporary images implies the rejection of any historicism in favour of an a-systematic inspiration, unpredictable and potentially *prophetic.*'[160] [Emphasis supplied] He further stipulates that 'abstraction cannot frighten the Christian if Christ himself, the Word made man, ..., did not hesitate to present himself in terms far from any possibility of figurative representation, like way, truth, life, and the light of men.'[161]

As prophetic painters we stand in a long tradition in the Christian church and can even see that modern Christian scholars acknowledge the ability of God to speak through art.

Graven Images

How, then, can we be allowed to paint concrete or abstract images? As previously stated, the Israelites did not paint very much. They painted on pottery and they dyed fabric and clothing. This is in part the result of the second commandment God gave the Israelites in Exodus 20:4-5:

> *You shall not make for yourself an image in the form of anything in heaven above or on the earth beneath or in the waters below. You shall not bow down to them or worship them; for I, the LORD your God, am a jealous God, punishing the children for the sin of the parents to the third and fourth generation of those who hate me.*

The word for idol or graven image is *pesel.* It means an image of a person or animal used to worship; a household god; an idol carved or fashioned from wood, stone, or metal.[162] We find this term 31 times in the Old Testament and each time it speaks about forbidden idol worship. In the other passages we see that people bow down to a graven image (Leviticus 26:1); that they corrupt themselves with idolatry (Deuteronomy 4:16); forget the covenant (4:23); and the result of making or worshiping a graven image is a curse (Deuteronomy 27:15) resulting in God's punishment (Exodus 20:5).

There is another Hebrew word that is often contrasted with *pesel:* which is *tselem,* and which we see in Genesis 1:26-27 when God created humans in His image, imago dei.[163] This term is used in 15 passages in the Old Testament - four times to speak about the image of God; seven times to speak of idols; 2 times to speak of sculptures of animals God used for healing (I Samuel 6:5 and 11); once to say that people put on a show (Psalm 39:6); and, once to speak about men looking into their own reflections (Psalm 73:20). We see that the use of *tselem* is not unambiguous, and we also see that the use of *pesel* is only for idols, and not for representations, sculptures, or paintings in general.

There is a second pair of Hebrew words which often get contrasted. In Exodus 20:4, God says that the Israelites should not make any 'likeness' of any thing. This term in the Hebrew is *temunah*. It comes from a root word that expresses something being apportioned, ie only looking at one part of it instead of the whole.[164] This is when we take something and make it an idol and we only focus on one aspect of it instead of on what it is in all its aspects. This term is found ten times in the Old Testament - five times in the same sense as Exodus 20:4; three times to describe a more general sense of likeness; one time to describe a vision (Job 4:16); and, one time to describe a reflection (Psalm 17:15). The word often contrasted with this is *demuth*. It is the likeness about which God spoke in Genesis 1:26; that He created humankind 'after our likeness.' This word does not mean focusing on one part, it means resemblance. We find it 22 times in the Old Testament. Four times it expresses likeness to God; twice, it speaks of a pattern or custom (II Kings 16:10 and Ezekiel 23:15); and, 18 times it shows that something resembles something else. Twelve of the last uses of the word occur in the book of Ezekiel alone. Again we see that the use of the terms is not completely unambiguous, but we can also gather that the ban on graven images and likenesses is related to idol worship.

If we look into the Tabernacle of Moses, we can see very clearly that God did not forbid any representation of nature as such. If He had, He would not have given Moses the instructions to build the Tabernacle and create the art in it in the way He did. There were many representations of both nature and the spiritual realm including palm trees, flowers, pomegranates, cherubim, and others.

Art in the Tabernacle of Moses

When we look into the art in the Tabernacle of Moses, we find that the creating of the Tabernacle, its furniture, fabrics, and perfumes, express, not only the making of images from nature, but also a host of creative expressions being used. The word for make, *asah*, is used many times in constructing and decorating the Tabernacle. It speaks of making furniture, as in Exodus 25:10, and poles in 25:13, as well as hammering out precious metal (25:17-18) and decorating furniture (25:25). In addition, creating dishes and vessels (25:29); shaping bowls like almond flowers (25:33-34); making curtains (26:1); weaving (26:1), and the making of coverings from animal skins (26:14). Finally, *asah* includes making wooden boards (26:15); making decorations in brass (27:4); making garments for the priests (27:2); creating chains (28:23); making the anointing oil asthe work of a perfumer (30:25), and making the incense a perfume (30:35). All these different creative expressions are included in the word *asah*. It is the same word used for the creation of man when God made man in His image in Genesis 1:26.

There are quite a few other words in these passages which describe some of the **creative processes** in more detail. First, we see *tsaphah*, meaning to overlay with metal or to cover with wood. It is used 39 times in the Old Testament. The first reference is in Exodus 25:11, for the Ark of the Covenant. Then comes *yatsaq*, translated as to cast metal, to stiffen fabric, or to pour liquids, used 53 times in the Old Testament. The first reference is in Exodus 25:12, for the gold rings used to make the carrying poles of the Ark. Another word is *miqshah*, meaning art work moulded by hammering. Pieces made in this technique are often hammered out of a single piece of precious metal, like the cherubim on top of the Ark of the Covenant (Exodus 37:7). It is used 9 times, the first reference being in Exodus 25:18. Then we see *tabniyth*, used to define a pattern, structure, form or likeness. It is used 17 times. The first reference to the pattern for the tabernacle is found in Exodus 25:9.

Next is *maaseh,* in general referring to an action, work, or deed. It also can refer to an occupation, a business, or possessions as well as to a purpose.[165] In connection with *raqam*, the embroiderer, it is defined 'needlework'[166] while in connection with *resheth* as 'network.'[167] The KJV translated it as an 'art' in several places.[168] Numbers 31:51 speaks of crafted jewels or gold, which is a phrase translated in the same manner to describe the brim of the sea made from cast metal in Solomon's Temple in I Kings 7:26. In II Kings 16:10, we find the word translated as 'workmanship' in the KJV, and in II Chronicles 4:6, it means an offering. *Maaseh* is found 220 times in the Old Testament. The first reference for the tabernacle is in Exodus 26:1 where it praises the 'cunning work' in which the cherubim are done in the curtains for the tabernacle. Cunning is used to describe the skill involved in these creative processes. The Hebrew word is *chashab*, a verb which means to plait or to weave. It appears 122 times in the Old Testament. It is the verb used to state that God 'counted' Abram's belief as righteousness (Genesis 15:6). Furthermore, we see the word *raqach*, meaning to perfume, to compound, or to make an ointment. We see it eight times in the Old Testament. The first time is in Exodus 30:25, regarding the oil with which the Tabernacle and the Ark need to be anointed.

We also see a famous word we have already looked at in Chapter Two, titled Art at the Centre of War, which is *charash*, designating the artisan or craftsman. There are 34 passages in the Old Testament that mention them. The first reference is in Exodus 28:11 where the term is translated as 'engraver.' Smith, carpenter, or mason are also trades mentioned in Exodus. Finally, the weaver, translated from *arag*, appears 13 times in the Old Testament, the initial time is in Exodus 28:32, where the decorative border around the robe of the ephod is woven.

I also want to look at a few words expressing wisdom, knowledge, and understanding in these passages in Exodus.

Tabun, means understanding and comes from a root verb meaning to separate mentally. It is also translated as to be cunning, to be eloquent, to be skillful, or to teach.[169] We find it 42 times in the Old Testament, three of which are in Exodus (31:3, 35:31, and 36:1). The first two times it conveys the understanding God gave to Bezalel and Oholiab as He filled them with His Holy Spirit to build the tabernacle and all its vessels, furniture, and artwork. The third time understanding is given by God to all the 'wise hearted' men to construct, establish and make everything for the tabernacle under Bezalel's and Oholiab's supervision.

Melakah, denotes workmanship and comes from the verb *malak* meaning to dispatch or to be a messenger.[170] This word is often translated as angel in the Old Testament. Workmanship includes the sense of being sent or having a message to bring. What a wonderful sense of calling as an artist that your workmanship can include bringing a message from God. *Melakah* is found 149 times in the Old Testament and is used to describe the 'work' God rested from on the seventh day (Genesis 2:2). It is first mentioned in relation to the tabernacle in Exodus 31:3 where it further explains what God put into Bezalel and Oholiab as He filled them with His Spirit.

Machashabah, meaning cunning works or work done with imagination. We find it in 52 passages in the Old Testament. Its root verb is *chashab* as previously mentioned. The first use is in Exodus 31:4 where God elaborated on the wisdom, knowledge and understanding He had given to Bezalel and Oholiab as He filled them with His Spirit.

Chokmah, is a word translated as wisdom, wit, or skill. It is wisdom in mind, word, or act. It occurs in 141 verses in the Old Testament. The first use is in Exodus 28:30 and involves the wisdom given to the 'wise hearted' men who will work with Bezalel and Oholiab.

There are also seven more terms which express other creative processes, including:

Chorosheth, which refers to cutting or carving. A similar process appears in I Kings 6:29 and 35, in which cherubim, palm trees, and flowers are carved in the temple of Solomon. The term here is *qala* which describes a circular motion used for the carving.

Kathab, describes writing or engraving. This verb is used for the process of engraving the tablets God gave Moses on Mount Sinai containing the Ten Commandments (Exodus 24:12 and 31:18). It also states that the tablets were written on or engraved by the finger of God.

Pathach, also means to carve or to engrave. We see it in Exodus 28:11 where the names of the tribes of Israel needed to be engraved on the two shoulder stones of the ephod. We also find the related word *pittuach*. It details a low or high relief, intaglio, or a carved work. These two words are used together in Zechariah 3:9, where the prophet speaks in a vision to Joshua the high priest. He prophesies about Jesus, as God's 'servant' or 'the branch.' The Lord shows Joshua a stone, representing Jesus (Ephesians 2:19-22). God says that He will carve an inscription on this stone and that as a result He will remove the sin from the land in one single day. There are various interpretations for the engravings on this stone, one being that it could be the names of those who are saved. They are written in the 'book of the lamb,' ie the 'book of life' (Malachi 3:16 and Revelation 3:5). They might also denote the suffering and wounds of Jesus which He endured to give us life. The land which will have its sin removed in a single day has often been interpreted as Jesus' land, the church (Ephesians 2:14).

Shabats is to interweave or to enchase gems in gold. It appears in Exodus 28:39 where the coat of the high priest is embroidered. The main word used for carving in the Old Testament is *miqlaath*. It appears in I Kings and describes the process of creating ornaments, flowers, cherubim, and palm trees. It probably stands for a technique we would call bas-relief today. Its root verb describes a circular motion, *qala*.[171] This word is used times in the Old Testament. Three times it is translated 'to carve'[172] and four times 'to sling'[173]. The latter translation is the one applied in I Samuel 17:49 to the motion David used to kill Goliath when he slung a pebble which struck the giant in his forehead and struck him dead. This same motion is the root verb which describes what artisans do when they carve or create bas-relief. Interesting?

Chaqaq, meaning to hack, to engrave, or to be a scribe, often appears when tablets are engraved with laws. One well known statement from the Old Testament also uses this verb: 'I have engraved you upon the palms of my hands' (Isaiah 49:16). Another use of the verb is in Ezekiel, Chapter Four, where we are told that prophecies were not only written or spoken, but also engraved, painted, or acted out.

Ezekiel 4

Ezekiel is a prophetic book full of visions. At the beginning of the book, the prophet is still in exile in Babylon. He had come to Babylon in the first wave of Israelites exiled from Judah. The book records six visions Ezekiel had between 593 and 571 BC. Chapter Four documents prophecies against Judah and Jerusalem. The prophet had spent time at Tel Abib (Ezekiel 3:15) and in the plain of the river Chebar (3:23). The Lord then ordered him to return to his house (3:24). This is where he receives the next prophetic command, which he acts out. I will not give a full interpretation of Ezekiel 4 now. There are many prophetic acts in this chapter, which will be addressed at a later stage. Now I will concentrate on the visual art in this chapter. In Ezekiel 4:1-2, God instructs the prophet:

> 'Now, son of man, take a block of clay, put it in front of you and draw the city of Jerusalem on it. Then lay siege to it: Erect siege works against it, build a ramp up to it, set up camps against it and put battering rams around it.'

God tells Ezekiel to take a tile, *lebeanh*. This word can also be translated as brick or white brick. This brick may have reminded the exiles of the bricks their forefathers made in slavery in Egypt. We see the same word for those bricks in Exodus 1:14. They were white or pale because of the clay used for them. These bricks were larger than our modern bricks. A tile or tablet of soft clay was used to write on, but this probably was a sun-baked brick on which the prophet scratched the outline of Jerusalem. This large visualisation of the city was part of the three-dimensional image which Ezekiel is told to set up in the following verses to enact the prophecies God is giving him.

Chaqaq, see above, is the word translated as draw, appears 19 times in the Old Testament. As laws were engraved or scratched into clay tiles, the word is often translated as lawgiver or governor. Can you see the implication that what Ezekiel did when he scratched or portrayed the outline of Jerusalem on the tile was the same process carried out when law was written on tablets? The implication here is of government. As he does this, is he giving a visual message from the One who gave the law? There is a deep connection between these two things in the word *chaqaq*; a deeper meaning which we need to be aware of when we paint or visualize a message from the Lord!

In Job 19:23, the KJV says 'printed in a book' whereas Isaiah 30:8 says 'inscribe it in a scroll.' Proverbs 8:27 and 29 uses the term to describe certain creative acts of God. Isaiah 22:16 describes the process of hewing a place to live out of rock.

Important keys in Scripture regarding painting, carving and engraving:

You shall not make for yourself an image in the form of anything in heaven above or on the earth beneath or in the waters below. You shall not bow down to them or worship them; for I, the LORD your God, am a jealous God, punishing the children for the sin of the parents to the third and fourth generation of those who hate me (Exodus 20:4-5).

Creative processes in the making of the Tabernacle in Exodus 25-28 and 30.

Engraving Jerusalem on a tile and performing a drama in Ezekiel 4.

Chapter Ten: Sculpture, Pottery, and Carpentry

That Snake

Many people draw a blank when I ask in one of my workshops where we see prophetic sculpture in the Bible. Some remember the golden calf, which is a sculpture but not an example of a message from the Lord. Others remember ashera poles and household idols which all fall into the same, negative, category. With a bit more time, someone usually remembers 'that snake', alluding to the bronze serpent God told Moses to sculpt. We find this quite bizarre story in Numbers 21:4-9:

> They traveled from Mount Hor along the route to the Red Sea, to go around Edom. But the people grew impatient on the way; they spoke against God and against Moses, and said, "Why have you brought us up out of Egypt to die in the wilderness? There is no bread! There is no water! And we detest this miserable food!"
>
> Then the LORD sent venomous snakes among them; they bit the people and many Israelites died. The people came to Moses and said, "We sinned when we spoke against the LORD and against you. Pray that the LORD will take the snakes away from us." So Moses prayed for the people.
>
> The LORD said to Moses, "Make a snake and put it up on a pole; anyone who is bitten can look at it and live." So Moses made a bronze snake and put it up on a pole. Then when anyone was bitten by a snake and looked at the bronze snake, they lived.

The people grumbled against God and Moses. In response, God sent venomous (or 'fiery') snakes which bit many people, who then died. This was an expression of judgement. When the Israelites repented in verse seven, Moses interceded for them and God told him to make a bronze snake and set it on a pole. Everyone who would look at it would live. So Moses made a fiery serpent and those who looked at it lived. Strange? Yes!

The word for venomous in verse six and the word for bronze snake in verse eight is the same Hebrew term, *saraph*. It comes from a root meaning to be on fire.[174] It says that fire was what the people experienced in their body after one of the snakes had bitten them. The word for bronze in verse nine is the Hebrew word *nechosheth*. We find the same term in Exodus 27:2 where the bronze altar in the tabernacle of Moses is described. This altar was for the burnt offerings and stands for justice and righteousness. This is where the prophetic meaning of the colour bronze or copper comes from - justice and righteousness. Taking these two passages of Scripture together we can interpret that the bronze snake was a symbol of making the people who looked at it, and submitted themselves to the verdict of the Lord, righteous again.

We see a sculpture of a snake on a pole being used to make people healthy again. What a strange symbol! We need to note here that God did not take the snakes away, as He could have done. He left them there and gave people the choice to repent, ie to look at a sculpture of the very thing that was bringing them death. Imagine this scene with people lying on the ground, and writhing in pain as fire is burning in them as the result of the snakebites. Moses put the pole with the snake up and even though all this commotion and death is occurring, people start looking at the pole and are healed. The writhing stops, people stop moving in pain, their countenance changes, slowly they get up again and break into joy as they realize that they live. Imagine this on a stage – what a drama!

You might ask how this sculpture was prophetic? We find the answer in John 3:14 where Jesus stated that the Son of Man must be lifted up as Moses lifted up the snake in the wilderness. Jesus said what

He did on the cross, another sculpture, was foretold in the sculpture of the bronze serpent. There are a few parallels here between Jesus and the serpent. Both were lifted up on a pole which, by the way, is the symbol for a curse in Deuteronomy 21:23. The Israelites had to look up towards the sculpture physically and the believer now lifts his or her eyes to Jesus spiritually. In both cases, life, in the first case physical, in the second eternal, is the result. Both the pole and the cross were images of a painful death. The pole showed the cause of death as a snake and the cross was a brutal Roman execution technique.

The sculpture in the wilderness, which God used to bring righteousness, healing and life, was clearly prophetic of the work of Jesus on the cross also bringing righteousness, healing and life. Moreover, it foreshadowed the fact that people have a choice. The Israelites had the choice to acknowledge the sculpture of the snake and be healed, while people today have the choice to acknowledge Jesus as the only way to God and to receive eternal life. God opens the way, but people have to choose to accept it.

Either sculpture, the pole with the snake or the cross with the Son of Man hanging on it, is absurd to the human mind, in the earthly realm. Nevertheless, in the heavenly realm and at the spiritual level, they represent the wisdom of God to bring salvation (I Corinthians 1:18-19). Jesus had to be lifted up on a symbol of a curse. In response to His obedience, His father lifted Him up, 'exalted him and gave him the name that is above every other name' (Philippians 2:9). This is our goal as artists. Our calling is to lift Jesus up in our prophetic art because the spirit of prophecy is the testimony of Jesus (Revelation 19:10).

God used the story of the bronze serpent to save the English preacher Charles H. Spurgeon (1834-1892). It happened on January 6, 1850, when Spurgeon was 15 years old. He was on his way to a church but was stopped by a snowstorm. He could not walk any further and turned into a street he had not intended to go into. He happened upon a small Methodist chapel with about a dozen people in attendance. When the minister, who was also stuck in the snowstorm, did not show up, a craftsman[175] spoke plainly and simply about Isaiah

45:22: 'Look unto me, and be saved, all the ends of the earth' (KJV). He spoke for about ten minutes about the necessity for people to look at Jesus to be saved. At the end of his talk, Spurgeon recalls, the man looked at him under the gallery. Let us follow Spurgeon's own words:

With so few people he knew me to be a stranger. Just fixing his eyes on me, as if he knew all my heart, he said, "Young man, you look very miserable." Well, I did, but I had not been accustomed to having remarks made from the pulpit on my personal appearance before. However, it was a good blow, struck right home. He continued, "and you always will be miserable – miserable in life and miserable in death – if you don't obey my text; but if you obey now, this moment, you will be saved." Then lifting up his hands, he shouted, "Young man, look to Jesus Christ. Look! Look! Look! You have nothing to do but to look and live." I saw at once the way of salvation. I know not what else he said – I did not take much notice of it – I was so possessed with that one thought. Like as when the brazen serpent was lifted up, the people only looked and were healed, so it was with me. I had been waiting to do fifty things, but when I heard that word, "Look!" What a charming word it seemed to me! Oh! I looked until I could have almost looked my eyes away.[176]

God used a simple craftsman to remind Spurgeon of the sculpture in the wilderness and the choice he had, which is to look to Jesus, and be saved.

We need to notice one more issue in the story of the bronze serpent. We read in II Kings 18:4 that King Hezekiah of Judah broke the bronze serpent into pieces because the Israelites burned incense to it, that is, they had made it an idol of worship. Nearly one thousand years had passed since Moses had made the serpent on a pole and it was still there. Imagine a piece of your art still existing after one thousand years. The problem here was that the Israelites had violated the second commandment God had given them; not to make graven images. They turned an image, which God called Moses to create, into a graven one and worshiped it. During his reforms, King Hezekiah destroyed it, and rightly so. We need to always be aware of who or what we worship - the Creator or the created thing. The first is always right and the latter is always wrong.

Altars

There are other three dimensional artefacts we should look at in Scripture to see prophetic sculpture. The people of Israel usually built these structures as places of worship, ie as places of sacrifice. All the words we find in both the Old and the New Testaments for altar describe places of sacrifice, with one exception.

The main word for altar in the Old Testament is *mizbeach*, which means a place of sacrifice. We see it in 338 verses in the Old Testament. We find another term, *madbach*, once in Ezra 7:17. It means a sacrificial altar. *Arieyl* is found twice in Ezekiel 43. It is a name for the altar in the Temple and thus means a place of sacrifice. One time, a figurative name is used for the altar of burnt offering, *herale*, in Ezekiel 43:15. It calls the altar of burnt offering 'the mountain of God.'[177] In the New Testament the word for altar is *thusiasterion*, meaning a place of sacrifice. We see it in 21 verses. The only exception is the altar for the unknown god in Acts 17:23. When Paul speaks to the men of Athens, he uses a different word for this altar, *bomos*, which literally means 'a stand.'[178] He clearly sees that this is not a place of sacrifice.

There are twelve places in the Old Testament where these altars were not only built to provide places of sacrifice, but also had a prophetic meaning. They are memorials of events and describe God as being the same yesterday, today, and forever. The twelve stones on the breastplate and the shoulder pieces of the ephod (Exodus 39:7) have the same function, which is, they are a memorial to the Lord.

In Genesis 12:7, God appears to Abram and gives him his calling. Abram builds an altar to the Lord to remember the promise of God. The altar has the function of reminding people who see it of the promise God gave and the prophecy given; 'to your offspring I will give this land'. In Genesis 22:9, Abraham builds an altar to sacrifice Isaac. The Lord provides a ram to sacrifice instead of Isaac. Abraham calls this altar *YHWH yireh* (verse 14), meaning 'The Lord sees' or

'The Lord provides.' It is a reminder of the fact that Abraham was obedient and God provided the goat to replace Isaac. In the following verses God blesses Abraham and prophesies that He will multiply his family and make them as numerous as the stars in the sky and the sand on the seashore. In Abraham's family all nations on earth will be blessed (verse 17-18).

In Genesis 26:25, Isaac builds an altar to the Lord after He had appeared to him and renewed His blessings on him. The altar reminds Isaac and his family of the renewal of the blessing and the future events God promised; 'I will increase the number of your descendants'. Isaac's son, Jacob, builds an altar in Genesis 33:20. After Jacob and Esau have met and reconciled, Jacob builds an altar to remind the generations to come that the God of Israel is a mighty God, *el elohey yisrael*. He builds another altar in Genesis 35:1-7 in the place where God had met him before, when he fled from Esau. This altar is called *el beythel*, meaning 'the God of the House of God.' The purpose of the altar was to remember that God had been with him when he was fleeing from his brother.

Moses builds an altar to the Lord in Exodus 17:15. The Israelites had defeated Amalek after Aaron and Hur had held up Moses' hands in intercession. The altar's name is *YHWH nissiy*, translated as 'The Lord is my banner' or 'The Lord is my sign of victory.' Moses also builds an altar and has twelve pillars or memorial stones set up for the twelve tribes. The altar commemorates the renewal of the covenant between God and Israel (Exodus 24:4-8). After the renewal of the covenant, Moses, Aaron, Nadab, and Abihu, together with seventy of the elders, go up the mountain to meet with the Lord. What happens next is a foreshadowing of the throne room in heaven. The men see God with His feet on something like sapphire stone that looks like the 'body of heaven' (verse 10). This corresponds to the description of the throne room in Revelation 4:3. They ate and drank with God (verse 11). The word translated as drank is the Hebrew word *shathah*. It also has the meaning of participating in a banquet.[179] This corresponds to the marriage feast of the Lamb in Revelation 19:9. Bezalel and his workmen also built the altar of burnt offering (Exodus 27:1-8) and the altar of incense (Exodus 30:1-10) in the Tabernacle of Moses. We will talk about these two and their prophetic meanings later.

The Lord directed Joshua to take twelve stones from the middle of the Jordan when the Israelites crossed the river (Joshua 4:1-7). One man from each tribe (verse 2) was to take a stone (verse 5) from the place in the middle of the river where the priests stood with the ark of the Covenant (verse three). The word altar is not used, but what Joshua built was an altar. It was there to remind people that the presence of the Lord had been with them (Joshua 3:8), parting the waters of the river (verse 7). Joshua also built an altar on Mount Ebal (Joshua 8:30-32).[180] He built this altar from unhewn stones (verse 31), which symbolize purity. He renewed the covenant and wrote a copy of the Law of Moses on the stones (verse 32).

In I Kings 18:20-40, Elijah confronted the prophets of Baal. He repaired the altar of the Lord that was broken down (verse 30) with twelve stones, one for each tribe of Israel (verse 31). He called the altar *yisrael*, meaning 'He will rule as God' (verse 31). You know the end of the story. At the time of the evening sacrifice, Elijah called out to God to let the people know that He was God in Israel (verse 36-37) and the fire of God fell (verse 38), consuming the sacrifice, the wood, the altar stones and the water in the trench (verse 38). Israel then returned to the Lord (verse 39).

The Israelites also had the tradition of erecting memorial stones. We see this in Genesis 28:18-22 where Jacob put the stone he had used as a pillow up as a pillar and called it *beythel*, 'the house of God.' He anointed it with oil and made a covenant with the Lord there.[181] He also made a covenant with Laban in Genesis 31:45-55. He set up a pillar and a heap of stones. Laban called it *yegar sahadutha*, 'to gather for witness,' while Jacob called it *galyed*, 'a heap of testifying.' Joshua renewed the covenant between God and Israel at Shechem and set up a great stone as a witness between God and the people (Joshua 24:27). After the Israelites had defeated the Philistines, Samuel took a stone and set it up between Mizpah and Shen (I Samuel 7:12). He called it *eben haezer*, meaning 'the Lord has helped us this far.'

These stones were visible, three-dimensional artefacts, which spoke to generations about what God had done in the past. They were there to remind the people of their heritage, as well as to teach them that their God was still the same God when they came across these 'sculptures' later. The Israelites were familiar with memorial stones and altars and they had people in their midst who worked with stones, whom they called *tekton*.

Jesus' Artisan Trade

We find the word *tekton* only twice in the New Testament (Matthew 13:55 and Mark 6:3); and both times it is applied to Jesus, describing his profession. There is widespread discussion regarding how to translate this term clearly. Suggested translations include carpenter, mason, master builder, architect, metal worker, joiner, artisan, craftsman, or artificer. He clearly had an artistic profession. The root word of this term also includes the connotation of being a teacher.[182] Depending on which Christian background people come from, they tend to either claim that Jesus was from a poor background, as his father was a simple carpenter, or that he was from a middle-class background and his father worked as an architect. We know that in 22 BC, King Herod had a gigantic temple built on what was left of Solomon's temple and that the Wailing Wall is the only part of it that still exists. People have claimed that 10,000 craftsmen were necessary to build such a structure. Can you imagine that Joseph, Jesus' earthly father, might have been involved in this project? We also know that from 6 AD to 19 AD, Herod Antipas rebuilt Sepphoris, the largest city in Judea outside of Jerusalem. Sepphoris was a few miles from Nazareth. Can you imagine that Joseph and his apprentice son were involved in the building work going on so close to their home town?

It is interesting to note that Jesus is described both in the Old and the New Testament as a stone. In Isaiah 28:16 God says that He will lay a stone in Zion; a foundation stone; a tried stone; and a precious corner stone (KJV). This is a tried stone as Jesus was tried before Pilate and then handed over to the soldiers. He is also called a precious or valuable corner stone. Peter reflects on this in his first letter (2:4-5):

As you come to him, the living stone – rejected by humans but chosen by God and precious to him – you also, the living stones, are being built into a spiritual house [dwelling or family] to be a holy priesthood, offering spiritual sacrifices acceptable to God through Jesus Christ.

Jesus is also called a living stone. He was resurrected and lives now and forever. He is called chosen by God and precious, because he is honoured and valuable. Peter builds on this description of Jesus as a stone and extrapolates it to include us, His followers, who also become living stones being built into a dwelling for God that will be a family. Jesus is the One who is building this family, His church (Matthew 16:18). He is the mason, the architect, and the head of the church. Remember, as you create, that you are following in the footsteps of the One who worked with wood and stone.

Both the Old and the New Testaments also describe God the Father as an artisan. Isaiah 64:8 says that God is our father, we are the clay and He is the potter. The Hebrew term for potter is *yatsar*. Its root meaning depicts someone who squeezes into form, someone who presses and who determines something.[183] In Jeremiah 18, God makes this very clear. Jeremiah was sent by God to the house of the potter. The potter made a vessel which was marred, so he kneaded the clay back together again and made another vessel out of the same clay. This was a prophetic act which explained to the people that God could deal with them in the same way (verse 6). As the clay was in the hand of the potter, so was Israel in God's hand. Job states in 10:9, that he is made from clay and that God has the power to return him to dust. We find the same relationship of the power of the maker over the material in Isaiah 29:16 and 45:9. With the same power, God moulded Adam from the dust of the ground (Genesis 2:7).

The term clay is the Hebrew word *chomer*. We see it 26 times in the Old Testament and nine times it is translated as 'clay'[184]. Its root meaning refers to something that is bubbling up.[185] This process happened when the potter kneaded the clay with his feet. The prophets and the people were familiar with these processes and knew where the potters worked. In his letter to the church in Rome, Paul cites this passage in the Old Testament and asks the church the same question (9:21): 'Does not the potter have the right to make out of the same lump of clay some pottery for special purposes and some for common use?' Clearly, God is portrayed as a potter who forms and moulds the clay according to His will.

The fact that Jesus today builds His dwelling and that God dwells in us, tabernacles with us,[186] was foreshadowed by the first dwelling place that God commanded Moses to build for Him during the wilderness years, which was the Tabernacle. The tent, its furniture and vessels had prophetic meaning. Let us discuss the Tabernacle, along with its furniture and vessels.

A Prophetic Dwelling Place

We can read about the Tabernacle and its contents in Exodus 25-27, 30-31, 35-38 and 40. In chapter nine, I previously wrote about the creative processes described in Exodus 25-28 and 30. There, we saw how the meanings of the words describing these various creative processes connect with other spiritual truths in Scripture. The Tabernacle, its furniture and vessels have many prophetic connections in Scripture as well, especially to the New Testament. They foretell of the coming of the Messiah. The Hebrew word for tabernacle is *mishkan*, which means place of dwelling. It describes a residence, albeit a portable one, while the Israelites wandered in the wilderness. The name denotes the manifest presence of God in the midst of His people, which God promised in Exodus 25:8: 'Then have them make a sanctuary for me, and I will dwell among them.' The term translated as among is *tavek*. It means in the centre and points to the New Testament fact that Jesus tabernacles among us (John 1:14). The Greek word translated as tabernacles or dwells is *skenoo*. It speaks of protection and communion. It points to the fact that we are now the temple of the living God in which He lives (II Corinthians 6:18).[187]

We can read the description of the Tabernacle in Exodus 26. There are many plans and reconstructions of the Tabernacle according to this description which one can find online and consequently

I will forgo describing the plan and construction of it. After Israel had crossed the Jordan into the Promised Land, the Tabernacle was in Gilgal, then Shiloh, and Bethel. After the ark of the Covenant was separated from the Tabernacle, it was located in Nob, and, finally, in Gibeon. From there the Tent of Meeting and all the sacred furnishings in it were brought into Solomon's temple (I Kings 8:4). We know nothing about what happened to it after the destruction of this temple by the Babylonians in about 587 BC. Let us now turn to the furnishings and vessels and their prophetic meaning.

1. The Altar of Burnt Offering

This altar is described in Exodus 27:1-5. It was made of acacia wood and overlaid with brass or possibly copper – the meaning of the Hebrew is difficult to be sure of in today's metallic terms. This is the place where the sacrifices were made to bring temporary atonement for sins (Leviticus 4, especially verses 4 and 18). The altar also had the 'eternal fire' on it (Leviticus 6:12-13). The ashes from the altar were to be brought outside of the camp (Leviticus 6:10-11). There is a lot of prophecy hidden in this basic information about the altar.

The fact that the altar was made of acacia wood and then overlaid with bronze is often interpreted to contrast humanity and divinity. It is thought to foreshadow the mystery of Jesus' humanity wrapped in His divinity. The wood stands for Jesus' humanity, the bronze or copper for His divinity. In this way, the altar prophetically speaks of Jesus being fully human and fully God (John 1:14). The altar of burnt offering is the visual representation of the forgiveness of sins. Copper as a material and colour, which symbolizes judgement, justice and forgiveness which come from God.

The altar provided the place for the sacrifices which had to be repeated again and again. The spilling of the blood and the burning of the sacrifice were necessary for atonement. The believer cannot come to God in his own righteousness. In a similar but final way, Jesus became the necessary sacrifice to bring us back into a right and full relationship with God. The sacrifices on the altar are a shadow of the 'once and for all' sacrifice of Christ (Hebrews 10:1-18 and I John 2:2).

The eternal fire on the altar reminded the priests of several things. First, the burning bush (Exodus 3) which was not burned up, and was a symbol of God's presence. The fire also reminded them of the pillar of fire in which God made His presence known at night (Exodus 13:21-22). Moses described God as a 'consuming fire' in Deuteronomy 4:24. This spoke of His holiness and presence. All these connotations were in the mind of the priests when they saw the altar of burnt offering. The fire spoke prophetically of a fire of justice (Matthew 3:12); of the baptism of fire Jesus gives us (Matthew 3:11 and Luke 3:16); of the Holy Spirit as a fire (Acts 2:3). Jesus' eyes are also a symbol of His essence, character and insight (Revelation 1:14, 2:18 and 19:12); of a fire of purification (Revelation 3:18); and, of God's presence (Revelation 4:5 and 15:2).

It is interesting to me that God even described a procedure for disposing of the ashes. They were not just dumped anywhere but instead in a clean place outside the camp. The ashes speak prophetically of a finished sacrifice. Jesus finished the work of atonement and restitution (John 19:30). He was crucified outside the city.[188] His sacrifice, which reconciled us to the Father, made Golgotha a place of cleansing. All these prophetic meanings are hidden in this piece of art, a three dimensional artefact, the altar of burnt offering.

2. The Laver or Washbasin of Bronze

Exodus 30:17-21 describes the washbasin made from bronze or copper and filled with water. The priests were to wash their hands and feet in it when they entered the tent of meeting and when they approached the altar of burnt offering. Throughout the Old and New Testaments water represents cleansing. The washbasin prophetically connotes baptism in water, foreshadowing repentance, cleansing and the resurrection to new life. Jesus described His Spirit, whom He will give to His followers, as 'a spring of water welling up to eternal life' (John 4:13). The washing of hands and feet also speaks prophetically of preparing the believers for service. This was the ritual the priests had to go through before serving the Lord. The hands speak of the things we do whereas the feet speak of the places where we do them.

Only the priests were allowed to use the washbasin as they were the only ones to approach the altar of burnt offering, foreshadowing that believers today need to cleanse themselves and need to be holy (I Peter 1:16), as a holy priesthood to the Lord (I Peter 2:5).

3. The Table of Showbread

This was a table with bread on it (Exodus 25:23-30 and Leviticus 24:5-6). It was made of acacia wood and overlaid with gold. The showbread is also called the 'bread of the presence' (Exodus 25:30). The term in Hebrew for the bread of the presence is *lechem paniym*, the first part meaning bread or loaf whereas the second part means 'the face'.[189] You could also translate this phrase as 'loaf of the face!' There are several other verses in the Old Testament where we see the same term. In Genesis 32:22-32, we see Jacob wrestling with God. What an encounter! He says in verse 30 that he had seen God 'face to face'; *paniym el paniym*. In Exodus 33:11, God speaks with Moses 'face to face' like a friend. The *lechem paniym* refers to the fact that the face of God is turned towards the place where the table is located. It also refers to communion with God and of entering into His presence which, in the Old Testament, was the privilege of the priests in the Holy Place. Exodus 25:29 tells us that the pitchers and bowls on the table were purposed for pouring out the drink offerings. Can you see that it prophetically foreshadowed communion as the table where God invites us to remember that Jesus' body was given for us and that His blood was shed for us? By this Jesus made a new covenant (I Corinthians 11:25) to bring us back into fellowship and communion with His Father.

In Numbers 4:7, the showbread is called the 'continual' bread. This is a reference to what Jesus said in John 6:51; 'I am the living bread that came down from heaven. Whoever eats this bread will live forever. This bread is my flesh, which I will give for the life of the world.' I am tempted to call the table of showbread installation art. Installation art is 'an artistic genre of three-dimensional works that are often *site-specific*… the term is applied to interior spaces.'[190] It can be installed either temporarily or permanently. In the case of the table of showbread, the installation was temporary as it was packed up again every time the Israelites moved from one place to another. Installation art integrates everyday and natural materials, ie a table, its dishes and the bread. These materials are 'often chosen for their "evocative" qualities.'[191] The bread and the dishes for the drink offerings were very evocative - even prophetic - as they prefigured the Lord's Supper, bringing strong images, memories or feelings to mind. We should not forget that a lamb was sacrificed on the altar of burnt offering every morning and evening in close proximity to the table of showbread. Do you see the image of the Passover meal appear as the priests were fulfilling their duties? Installation art involves a sensory experience, which we can also see in the table of showbread, the sacrifice of the lambs, and the drink-offerings. If one wants to understand which type of installation art the table of showbread was, I would put it in the category of a mobile-based interactive installation. Interactive installations 'involve the audience acting on the work of art.'[192]

4. The Lampstand or the Menorah

Exodus 25:31-40 give a detailed profile of the menorah. It was a huge sculpture which functioned as a lampstand with seven oil lamps. It had six branches with three cups shaped like almond flowers on each of them as well as almond buds and blossoms. It was one mass hammered out of pure gold (verse 31). Jewish oral tradition gives the height of it as approximately 1.6 metres. The lamps on it were filled with pure olive oil and burned from evening until morning (Exodus 27:21). The middle light was called the 'eternal light,' *ner Elohim*, as it was supposed to burn continually according to Exodus 27:20. The menorah has become a symbol of Judaism and is the emblem on the coat of arms of the modern state of Israel.

The history of the menorah can be traced through the Tabernacle of Moses, the first and the second temple, from which it was taken to Rome after the destruction of Jerusalem in 70 AD. It was displayed as a war trophy in the Temple of Peace in Rome. Emperor Vespasian[193] had it built to show his power and divinity. He also decorated the interior of the temple and the neighbouring buildings with loot from

Jerusalem and the second temple. After 455 AD when Rome had been taken by the Vandals, its fate is unknown. A depiction of the menorah can be seen on the south inner panel of the Arch of Titus in Rome. The Arch was constructed to memorialize the deification of Titus and his victory over the Jews in 70 AD together with his father, Vespasian. The menorah was the centre of attraction of the panel and carved in deep relief.

What does the menorah stand for prophetically? When one looks at the form of the menorah, it can remind us of a tree with branches – specifically, the Tree of Life (Genesis 2:9 and Revelation 22:2). The text in Exodus speaks of the menorah's 'branches,' translated from *qaneh*. This Hebrew term is used in 38 verses in the Old Testament. In Genesis 41:5 and 22, it is translated as a 'stalk' of corn when Pharaoh shares his dream with Joseph. Isaiah 42:3 tells us the Lord's chosen servant, Jesus, will not break a bruised 'reed' nor snuff out a smoldering wick. *Qaneh* comes from a root word, *qanah*, which means to create, to buy, to possess or to attain.[194] In Nehemiah 5:8, the term is translated as 'redeemed' (KJV). Psalm 74:2 speaks of God 'purchasing' the nation of Israel and Isaiah 11:11 says that the Lord will 'recover' (KJV) or 'reclaim' the remnant of His people from the nations. Jesus compares the believers to branches in John 15:5, where He calls Himself the true vine.

The seven lamps have a spiritual connection to the seven spirits in front of the throne of God.[195] The light on the menorah makes a prophetic connection to Jesus being the light of the world (John 8:12 and 9:5). John 1:9 describes Jesus as 'the true light.' It also stands for the fact that God's light will arise over Israel and that the nations will come to her light (Isaiah 60:1-3). The fact that the Holy Place was only illuminated by the light of the menorah and not by natural light, can be interpreted as the believer's illumination in faith coming from the Lord through the disclosure of the Holy Spirit (John 16:13).

The cups on the menorah prophetically connote the cup Jesus was to drink from (Matthew 20:22) by shedding His blood on the cross. Jesus asked for this cup to be taken from Him, if possible, but surrendered to the Father's will (Matthew 26:39). It is the cup He took when instituting the celebration of communion (Luke 22:14-23). The cup symbolizes a drink-offering; surrender to God's will; suffering and death; and, the new covenant Jesus made in His blood.

The menorah was also featured in a vision recorded by the prophet Zechariah. He was a contemporary of Haggai under the reign of King Darius the Great[196] of Persia. The first group of Jewish exiles had left Babylon in 538 BC and were still in the process of rebuilding the temple against much opposition when Zechariah shared his vision.

Chapter 4 verses 1 through 6 read:

Then the angel who talked with me returned and woke me up, like someone awakened from sleep. He asked me, "What do you see?" I answered, "I see a solid gold lampstand with a bowl at the top and seven lamps on it, with seven channels to the lamps. Also there are two olive trees by it, one on the right of the bowl and the other on its left." I asked the angel who talked with me, "What are these, my lord?" He answered, "Do you not know what these are?" "No, my lord," I replied. So he said to me, "This is the word of the LORD to Zerubbabel: 'Not by might nor by power, but by my Spirit,' says the LORD Almighty.

The menorah in this vision has a bowl over it with seven channels to the lamps. This part of the vision declares that the rebuilding of the temple will in the end be successful, but that it will not come about through human effort, but through the Spirit of the Lord. It is an encouragement to the returned exiles and also a prophetic foreshadowing of Jesus building His followers into a new temple.

In Chapter 4, verses 11 to 14 of Zechariah, it says,

Then I asked the angel, "What are these two olive trees on the right and the left of the lampstand?" Again I asked him, "What are these two olive branches beside the two gold pipes that pour out golden oil?" He replied, "Do you not know what these are?" "No, my lord," I said. So he said, "These are the two who are anointed to serve the Lord of all the earth.

There are many interpretations of the two olive trees, especially in connection with Revelation 11:4. To explore these explanations, which are very varied and, in my opinion, often speculative, would go well beyond the scope of this book. Suffice to say that they prophetically speak of the Holy Spirit. We can also see that the menorah was a three-dimensional artefact, and a prophetic sculpture, which had a major function in the Holy Place.

The menorah also plays a major part in the story of Hanukah. This is a Jewish festival celebrating the rededication of the second Temple during the Maccabean Revolt[197]. The story goes that after the army of Seleucid King Antiochus IV, who held the title *epiphanes* meaning 'God manifest,' was ousted from the temple, it was discovered that only one container of consecrated olive oil for the lamps on the menorah was left. This would have been only enough oil to keep the lamps burning for one day. Miraculously, the lamps burned for eight days which was the time span required to produce new, consecrated oil. To commemorate the miracle of the oil, Jews today light the Hanukah menorah. Part of the traditional meal during the celebration is to eat foods fried or baked in oil.

5. The Altar of Incense

Exodus 30:1-10 describes the second altar as the altar of incense. It was built of acacia wood and overlaid with gold. It was used to burn incense during the times of the morning and evening sacrifices, when the priest tended to the lamps in the morning and lighted them again in the evening (Exodus 30:7-8). The incense prophetically speaks of the prayers of the believers (Psalm 141:2, Revelation 5:8 and 8:3-4). The altar is also interpreted as a prophetic foretelling of the continual intercession of Jesus for the believers (Romans 8:34 and Hebrews 7:25).

6. The Ark of the Covenant and the Mercy Seat

The ark is depicted in detail in Exodus 25:10-22. It was a box made from acacia wood, overlaid with gold. It was placed in the Holy of Holies and contained the two stone tablets with the Ten Commandments, Aaron's rod and a jar of manna. On top of it was the mercy seat with two winged cherubim, made from a mass of pure gold. It was the place where God's presence rested. He said that this was the place where He would meet with the people and commune with them (verse 22).

Exodus 37:1 states that Bezalel made the ark himself. It was carried by the Israelites into the promised land and was then kept at Bethel and Shiloh. At the battle of Eben Ezer and Aphek it was captured by the Philistines, who kept it at Ashdod, Gad and Ekron. After its return to Israel, it was kept at Beth-Shemesh and Kirjath-jearim from which King David brought it to Jerusalem. On the journey it was in the house of Obed-Edom for three months. From David's tabernacle it went into the second Temple which was destroyed in 587 BC. Nothing is known of the ark after that date. Many scholars interpret the fact that the ark was made from acacia wood and overlaid with gold as a prophetic symbol of believers becoming the temple of the Holy Spirit in the New Covenant (I Corinthians 6:19). The place where God's presence rests is made of the believers in Jesus.

The Ten Commandments were the first portion of the Law given by God. They represent the beginning of the covenant He made with the Israelites at Mount Sinai. They were the foundation for a new society that was very different from those of the surrounding nations. This foreshadows the new society of which Jesus preached as the 'kingdom of God' (Mark 1:14-15). This kingdom and its righteousness are what we are called to seek first (Matthew 6:33). The Ten Commandments were a covenant text preparing the way for the New Covenant in Jesus (Hebrews 8:10), of which the prophet Jeremiah (31:33) already spoke. Christ came to fulfill the law (Matthew 5:17). The term translated as fulfill is *pleroo*. We also see this verb in Ephesians 5:18 in which it says: 'Be filled [again and again to overflowing] with the Spirit.' *Pleroo* is a verb which means that something is getting so full that it overflows in the process. It can also be translated as being crammed, packed, teeming, bursting or brimming.[198] In this sense, Jesus fulfills the law, that is He brings it to perfect fruition in us, which is something we are unable to do without Him.

The story of Aaron's rod is told in Numbers 17. After the rebellion of Korah God showed that Aaron and his sons, as representatives of the tribe of Levi, were selected to lead Israel in priestly service. Moses placed twelve rods in front of the ark overnight and only Aaron's had budded in the morning. It showed buds, blossoms and fruits (almonds). This confirmed Aaron's leadership and authority among the priests. The buds, blossoms and almonds prophetically speak of resurrection life and point to the resurrection of Jesus as the first of the royal priesthood (I Peter 2:9). Jesus is the high priest of the New Covenant (Hebrews 4:14). He holds all authority in heaven and on earth (Matthew 28:18) and sends us out in the great commission to exercise this authority.

The jar of manna was a reminder to the Israelites of their dependence on God, showing God's provision. In John 6:31-40, Jesus speaks of the manna in the desert and calls it 'bread from heaven.' He then explains that the one who comes down from heaven is the bread of God and the bread of life. Bread was a staple food in Biblical times and a symbol of life. In the Lord's Prayer (Matthew 6:11), 'bread' is the synonym for provision. It describes a relationship of trust with the Lord. Bread is also the symbol for Jesus' body broken for us in the Lord's supper.

The mercy seat relates to Jesus and His work. In Romans 3:25, Paul writes about Jesus being purposed by God to be the 'propitiation' (atonement) by which we are made righteous. The Greek term translated as propitiation is *hilasterion.* This word is used in the Septuagint for the mercy seat. The Hebrew word for the mercy seat, *kaphar,* is a primitive root, which expresses to make atonement, to cleanse, to forgive and to reconcile.[199] The cherubim represent the judgement of God, which is averted by the yearly sprinkling of blood on the Day of Atonement, and also explains Jesus' perfect sacrifice for us. It was the lid or cover for the ark and fit perfectly on it. Jesus is the perfect sacrifice! His love covers a multitude of sin (I Peter 4:8). There was no wood in the mercy seat which prophesies that forgiveness purely comes from Jesus. We cannot do anything in our own power to bring it about.

The ark of the Covenant and the mercy seat together are a prophetic artefact that foretells of the believers becoming the temple of the Holy Spirit. It also foreshadows the coming of the kingdom of God and the fulfilling of the law by Jesus; challenges us as royal priests to exercise our authority; and, it declares God's provision and Jesus' perfect sacrifice. The furniture in the tabernacle and their furnishings and vessels bear prophetic significance. They are prophetic artefacts, sculptures and installations, which point us to the New Covenant and the coming of the Messiah.

Important keys in Scripture regarding sculpture, pottery and carpentry:

When they reached the place God had told him about, Abraham built an altar there and arranged the wood on it. Abraham looked up and there in a thicket he saw a ram caught by its horns. He went over and took the ram and sacrificed it as a burnt offering instead of his son. So Abraham called that place The LORD Will Provide (Genesis 22:9a and 13-14a).

'Moses built an altar and called it The LORD is my Banner' (Exodus 17:15).

The making of the Tabernacle, and its furniture and vessels in Exodus 25-27, 30-31, 35-38 and 40.

The LORD said to Moses, "Make a snake and put it up on a pole; anyone who is bitten can look at it and live." So Moses made a bronze snake and put it up on a pole. Then when anyone was bitten by a snake and looked at the bronze snake, they lived (Numbers 21:8-9).

Then Elijah said to all the people, "Come here to me." They came to him, and he repaired the altar of the LORD, which had been torn down. Elijah took twelve stones, one for each of the tribes descended from Jacob, to whom the word of the LORD had come, saying, "Your name shall be Israel." Then the fire of the LORD fell and burned up the sacrifice, the wood, the stones and the soil, and also licked up the water in the trench. When all the people saw this, they fell prostrate and cried, "The LORD—he is God! The LORD—he is God! (I Kings 18:30-31 and 38-39).

'[King Hesekia] broke into pieces the bronze snake Moses had made, for up to that time the Israelites had been burning incense to it. (It was called Nehushtan)' (II Kings 18:4b).

'Isn't this the carpenter's son?' (Matthew 13:55a).

As you come to him, the living Stone—rejected by humans but chosen by God and precious to him— you also, like living stones, are being built into a spiritual house to be a holy priesthood, offering spiritual sacrifices acceptable to God through Jesus Christ (I Peter 2:4-5).

Chapter Eleven: Prophetic Writing

God Writes

I want to start by stating that God writes. He inscribed the original tablets He gave to Moses on Mount Sinai with the Ten Commandments (Exodus 31:18 and 32:15-16) and on the replacements after Moses had broken the original ones (Exodus 34:1). God also writes in the book of life which is very prophetic as He writes things in it before they happen[200]. God also wrote a prophecy on the wall of the palace of King Belshazzar of Babylon (Daniel 5). The prophecy appeared as soon as the king, his nobles, his wives and his concubines drank from the golden vessels his father had stolen from the first temple in Jerusalem, and as soon as 'they praised the gods of gold and silver, of bronze, iron, wood and stone' (Daniel 5:4). God wrote the prophecy on the wall as a response to defiling the holy vessels and to idolatry. The prophecy spoke of the King's death because of his pride. It was fulfilled 'that very night' (Daniel 5:30).

God also sent 'a man clothed in linen who had a writing kit [an inkhorn] at his side' to Jerusalem in Ezekiel 9. The man marks all those in Jerusalem, who 'grieve and lament over all the detestable things that are done in it' (9:4). Only these lived and escaped the judgement God poured out over Jerusalem in this vision. This writing was prophetic and decided between life and death. God puts the same mark on the heart of the people when He makes His covenant with them (Isaiah 31:33, Hebrews 8:10 and 10:16). He even writes the requirement of the law on the hearts of gentiles (Romans 2:15). Paul reminds us in II Corinthians 3:1-3 that we, as followers of Jesus, are living letters from Christ, 'written not with ink but with the Spirit of the living

God, not on tablets of stone but on tablets of human hearts' (3:3). In Jeremiah 17:1, God says that Judah's sin is engraved on the tablets of their hearts. Ask yourself: What is engraved on the tablet of your heart? Are there things that oppose each other, such as things written on your heart by the Lord *and* by sin? What do you read on your heart when you create? In Ezekiel 9:4, the answer to this question was a matter of life and death. Is there anything you need to do about this?

People Write

Most writing in the times of the Old Testament was done by scribes. They were the main group or class in Israel who were able to read and write. They wrote down the law, annals and records, legal documents, agreements and letters. They enjoyed considerable authority based on their skills. Baruch the scribe, for instance, wrote down the words of the prophet Jeremiah at his command (Jeremiah 36: 4-8). They wrote on scrolls, tablets and stone. In New Testament times we also see parchments and sheep skins as writing materials. The Hebrew term for scribe is *saphar* or *sapher*. It comes from a root that means to inscribe. The fact that they knew how to write was often equivalent to having knowledge and understanding. Jonathan, King David's uncle, is called a 'counsellor,' a 'wise man' and a 'scribe' in I Chronicles 27:32. Scribes were called upon to interpret the law and to teach, as we see in Nehemiah 8:8. 'During the Talmudic period the roles of the scribe and the wise were assimilated into the title Rabbi.'[201]

Manuscripts of the law and the prophets were often 'vocalized, accented and sometimes illuminated',[202] which illustrates the artistry among the scribes. Scribes were 'artisans of the highest caliber.'[203] They underwent extensive training and had to follow strict rules when copying the law. The process of copying was so important that it got codified in the Talmud. You can find more detail about this in Appendix 3. Scribes were not only responsible for copying, transmitting and interpreting the law, but they also had a more general responsibility for the language. They were the ones who passed writing on from one generation to the next. In a similar fashion, Martin Luther, (1483-1546) took responsibility for the German language when he translated the Bible into German in 1522 (New Testament) and 1534 (Old Testament and Apocrypha). Luther established a homogeneous style for the language which was close to the dialect spoken at the Saxon court and also understandable to people in both the North and the South of the German speaking states. There was no common German language at the time, only many different dialects.

Ezra, one of the foremost scribes in the Old Testament, returned from the Babylonian exile and reintroduced the law in Jerusalem. He is called a priest[204] and a scribe (Ezra 7:6). It is interesting to notice that both functions come together in one person. Today, as followers of Christ, we are a royal priesthood (I Peter 2:9) and we are called to 'make disciples of all nations, baptizing them in the name of the Father and of the Son and of the Holy Spirit, teaching them to observe all that I [Jesus] have commanded you' (Matthew 28:19-20). Do you see the connection? As followers of Jesus we are called to be priests and to pass on the Gospel to others. When you share Jesus through your life and your creativity, not only when you write, you fulfil the calling of a scribe in modern terms. Jesus addressed the scribes of His times directly in Matthew 13:52:

'Therefore every scribe who has become a disciple in the kingdom of heaven is like a head of a household, who brings forth out of his treasure things new and old.'

This is the last of seven parables[205] Jesus speaks in Matthew 13. I recognize that Jesus addressed this parable to a specific group of people, the scribes of His time. I think, however, that we can also look at this parable from a slightly different angle: as we are disciples in the kingdom of heaven, we also are called to bring out of our treasure, which is our hearts[206] - things both new and old. We are called to spread the truths we have long known and the truths we are currently learning from Jesus. We have to stand on the law which was fulfilled by Jesus and on the work of the Spirit who speaks and creates through us today. John gave a fine explanation of things new and old in his first letter (2:7-8):

Dear friends, I am not writing you a new command but an old one, which you have had since the beginning. This old command is the message you have heard. Yet I am writing you a new command; its truth is seen in him and in you, because the darkness is passing and the true light is already shining.

These treasures both new and old are sometimes pent up in us and need to come out. They need to be birthed. God's truth was in Jeremiah's heart 'like a fire shut up in [his] bones' (Jeremiah 20:9). He could not hold it in. Do you sometimes feel that God's truth is shut up in your bones and you need to release it? To let it out? While I lived and studied in South Africa with Youth With A Mission in Muizenburg in 2008, our team went on outreach to Zambia. There was a popular song about the fire shut up in the bones at that time which we used to choreograph a warfare dance. We danced it in several strategic places in Zambia, one of which being Niamkolo church, the oldest stone church in Zambia near Mpulungu. In this case, we danced the truth that we could not contain. Others have written about it, painted it, sculpted it, sung it, and composed it. Treasures both new and old come in many expressions. We need to be ready to express them. As written in Psalm 45:1: 'My tongue is the pen of a ready writer.' Tongue in the Hebrew is *lashown*, which also means language or tongue of fire.[207] Ready in the Hebrew is *mahiyr*. It comes from a root which means to flow easily and is translated as skilled, trained or speeding a cause![208] Are you trained in your skills and ready to flow easily as God asks you to spread the truth He has put into you? Do you have a tongue of fire which is under God's discipline so that you can bring itout, in writing or other expressions of truths, both new and old? Do you speak the language of the people God calls you to address through your creativity?

Prophetic Writing

There are many prophecies in the Old and New Testaments. You will be familiar with the writings of the Major Prophets (Isaiah, Jeremiah, Ezekiel and Daniel) as well as the Minor Prophets (Hosea, Joel, Amos, Obadiah, Jonah, Micah, Nahum, Habakkuk, Zephaniah, Haggai and Malachi). These books of the Bible are full of prophecies, of course, but there are other books of the Bible which contain prophecies, including Genesis, Numbers, Deuteronomy, II Samuel, Job, Psalms,

Matthew, I Corinthians, I Thessalonians and Revelation. It would far exceed the scope of this book to give even an overview of all the prophecies contained in the Bible. Many books have been written on this subject. I would like to mention, however, one early prophecy in Genesis 3 as it is often seen by scholars as the first mention of the gospel and as the first messianic prophecy in the Old Testament:

'And I will put enmity between you and the woman, and between your seed and hers; he will crush your head and you will strike his heel.'

This passage is called the protoevangelium. It is derived from two Greek words meaning 'first' and 'good news.' The seed of the woman is usually interpreted as Jesus and the bruising of the heel as the crucifixion. The crushing of the serpent's head is usually interpreted as the destruction of the devil, which began with the crucifixion and ends when he is thrown into the lake of fire (Revelation 20:10). In Romans 16:20, Paul refers to the protoevangelium stating that 'God, the source of shalom, will soon crush the Adversary under your feet' (CJB). Here, the seed of the woman is the church under the headship of the God of Shalom, whose feet which will crush the enemy.

What about prophetic writing today? Paul wrote to the church in Corinth that 'you can all prophesy in turn' during the meeting (I Corinthians 14:31). If someone utters a prophetic word, a word of encouragement or a word of wisdom today, and writes it down, it is prophetic writing. There are people who write prophetically occasionally; there are people who write prophetically often. There are specific times when people receive things to write from the Sprit, short or long prose or poems. All this is prophetic writing, although not at the esteemed level of Scripture. Some people have a burden to write like in Habakkuk 2:2. The fact that a piece of writing has been received under the influence of the Spirit or in the presence of God, does not mean that it might not need to be edited and checked against the Bible (I Thessalonians 5:20-21). Humility is a good guide in this process (James 4:10). Again, you can find many books written about prophetic writing or writing in the Spirit. You can find some recommended books in the *Suggested Reading* section.

Prophetic Poetry

I have already mentioned prophetic poetry. When I think of poetry in the Bible I usually think of the book of Psalms first. But there are other books of poetry, such as Job, Proverbs, Ecclesiastes, Song of Songs and Lamentations. We also find short passages of poetry in other books of the Bible. These passages are found in the blessings of Jacob's sons (Genesis 49); the song of Moses (Exodus 15:1-18); the song of Deborah and Barak (Judges 5); and, David's eulogy for Saul and Jonathan (II Samuel 1:19-27), to name just a few.

Scholars divide Hebrew poetry into three types[209] which include, 'lyric poetry' being sung to music as in the Psalms; 'didactic poetry' conveying maxims of life as in Proverbs and Ecclesiastes; and, 'dramatic poetry' using discourse to get its points across as in Job and the Song of Songs. Among lyrical poetry, we can distinguish between a *shir*, simply meaning a song; a *mizmor*, meaning a worship song; a *qina*, usually an eulogy; a *tehilla*, often a new song; and, a *mashal*, a proverb or satire.[210] Hebrew poetry works with parallelism and figures of speech[211]. It does not have rhythm or metre that we are used to in Western poetry today.

Prophetic poetry also often contains a foretelling of events. Looking again into poetic passages of the Old Testament outside of the book of Psalms, we can see prophetic poetry in Genesis 49, Exodus 15:12-17, Judges 5:31 and II Samuel 1:21, to name a few. Let us now turn to the main poetical book of the Bible, the book of Psalms.

Psalms

Please remember what I wrote in the section 'Psalms – Poems Set to Notes' in chapter eight entitled Prophetic Music about the authorship of the Psalms, their types and content. I focused on the Psalms as music, so now I will discuss the Psalms as prophetic poems. Psalm 45:1 brings out this connection between writing (poems) and singing (music) in a beautiful way, by reading 'My tongue is the pen of a skillful writer.' In Psalm 71:28, David vows that he will declare God's power and His mighty acts 'to all who are to come.' David's declaration has been preserved because he wrote it down. He was called a prophet by Peter (II Peter 2:30) and David knew that he was a prophet as he expressed in his last words (II Samuel 23:2). This means that the Psalms have a prophetic purpose for us today.

There are many prophecies in the Book of Psalms, especially about Jesus as the Messiah. Right now I want to point out just a few critical ones: Jesus was not to see corruption (Psalm 16:10 and Acts 2:31, 13:35); Jesus is the good shepherd (Psalm 23:1 and John 10:11, I Peter 2:25); not one of His bones was broken at the cross (Psalm 34:20 and John 19:31-36); He was given vinegar for His thirst (Psalm 69:21 and Matthew 27:34); and, He taught in parables (Psalm 78:1-2 and Matthew 13:34-35). I selected these verses just to give you an idea that prophecies about Jesus are scattered throughout the Psalms, and not concentrated in one or two areas. Still, I want to look at three Psalms which usually are considered to be messianic: Psalm 2, Psalm 22 and Psalm 110. A messianic Psalm is one considered to be prophetic in predicting the coming of the Messiah despite the fact that it would have had a contemporary meaning at the time it was written.

Please read Psalm 2: The writer tells of the nations conspiring against YHWH and His Messiah in verse 2. As the believers pray in Acts 4:24-30, they apply the first two verses of this Psalm to Herod, Pontius Pilate, the Gentiles and the people of Israel conspiring against the Lord and His anointed one, Jesus. The Psalmist goes on in verses 7-8 to speak about the son of the Lord who is begotten, which is yalad in Hebrew. It means to give birth, to show lineage and to be the son of someone.[212] The verb is used in the grammatical form called qal which signifies a causal action. We find the corresponding statements about Jesus being the 'begotten' son in the writing of John[213] where monogenes or its root gennao is used. It denotes a parent-child relationship and the fact that the child is a single one of its kind. The fact that Jesus is the begotten son is also part of the Creed of most Christian confessions.

In a contemporary context, this could have been King David as God called him His son in the Davidic covenant (II Samuel 7:14-15) or it could have been Israel (Exodus 4:22). Jesus is declared God's son in Matthew 3:17 and 17:5. Verse 7 of Psalm 2 is directly quoted in Acts 13:33 where the fact that He is God's son is connected with His resurrection. Verse 9 speaks of the son breaking the nations with an iron rod and smashing them to pieces like pottery. Jesus tells John in His prophecy against Thyatira;

> *to the one who is victorious and does my will to the end, I will give authority over the nations – that one "will rule them with an iron scepter and will dash them to pieces like pottery" – just as I have received authority from my Father.*

Psalm 2:9 is also quoted in Revelation 12:5 where the woman gives birth to a son, and in Revelation 19:15 where Jesus is portrayed as the rider on the white horse.

Please read Psalm 22: David writes in this Psalm about being a worm; being surrounded by bulls; roaring lions; being poured out like water; and, his heart being melted like wax, to name just a few figures of speech. This Psalm is striking in how it calls attention to the crucifixion of Jesus. Psalm 22 and Isaiah 53 formed a significant basis for the understanding of Jesus' crucifixion in the New Testament church. Jesus cried out verse 1 of Psalm 22 while He was being crucified (Matthew 27:46). Verses 6-18 seem like a description of the crucifixion. Let us look briefly at the corresponding verses:

Psalm 22:6 corresponds to Isaiah 53:3 (Jesus despised and mocked).

Psalm 22:7 corresponds to Luke 18:32-33 (Jesus mocked).

Psalm 22:8 corresponds to Luke 23:35 (Let Jesus save himself).

Psalm 22:14 corresponds to Matthew 26:38 (Jesus' soul overwhelmed).

Psalm 22:15 corresponds to John 19:28 (Jesus being thirsty).

Psalm 22:16 corresponds to Mark 15:25 (Jesus' hands and feet pierced).

Psalm 22:17 corresponds to Luke 23:35 (People watching Jesus' crucifixion).

Psalm 22:18 corresponds to John 19:23-24 (Jesus' clothing being divided by lot).

We can see how unbelievably clearly Psalm 22 conveys the crucifixion!

Hebrews 2:12 quotes Psalm 22:22 and says that Jesus is not ashamed to call us His brothers and sisters. The term which the writer of Hebrews uses as brothers and sisters in the quotation is the Hebrew word *ach*, brother, which has been translated as brothers, my people and my community in various English translations.

Please read Psalm 110: Jesus spoke about Psalm 110:1 to the Pharisees in Matthew 22:41-46 and established that David speaks about the Messiah in the Psalm's passage. Jesus was taken up into heaven and sits at the right hand of God. This fact is mentioned at least 18 times in the New Testament,[214] which demosntrates the significance of this prophecy that Jesus fulfilled.

Verse four declares the Messiah to be 'a priest forever in the order of Melchizedek.' Melchizedek was the King of Salem [Jerusalem] and a priest of the Most High God. He brought bread and wine, a foreshadowing of the last supper and of communion, to Abram after his defeat of Kedorlaomer and the kings allied with him, and blessed Abram (Genesis 14:18-20). This verse is applied to Jesus by the writer of Hebrews (5:6-10, 6:20 and all of chapter 7). If we look at how much is written about this in Hebrews, we see again how significant a prophecy we find in Psalm 110.

As I said before, there are many prophecies in the Book of Psalms, and not only about Jesus. Many of them are couched in poetry, in figures of speech, and expressed in parallelism. To shine a bit more light on these facts, let us turn to some examples.

Please Read Psalm 80: It is addressed to the Shepherd of Israel. Jesus calls Himself the good shepherd in John 10:11. You can say that the Psalm is addressed to Jesus! It is a Psalm about national destruction and restoration. It is full of figures of speech. The main one refers to Israel as a vine, which God transplanted from Egypt and gave the promised land to where it 'took root and filled the land' (verse nine). 'The mountains were covered with its shade, the mighty cedars with its branches. Its branches reached as far as the Sea, its shoots as far as the River' (verses 10 and 11). But Israel gets destroyed and is described as 'Your vine is cut down, it is burned with fire' (verse 16). Read verses five and six again which says 'You have fed [your people] with the bread of tears; you have made them drink tears by the bowlful. You have made us an object of derision to our neighbours, and our enemies mock us.' The Hebrew word translated as derision is madon. It also means strife, discord or brawling.[215] These two verses remind me of what happened to the Jewish people during the Holocaust. Not everyone might see this connection, but I think these verses speak prophetically about an event which happened over three thousand years after they were written. When I read Psalm 83:1-8 I am reminded of the Holocaust again, where it is written:

O God, don't sit idly by, silent and inactive when we pray. Answer us! Deliver us! Don't you hear the tumult and commotion of your enemies? Don't you see what they are doing, these proud men who hate the Lord? They are full of craftiness and plot against your people, laying plans to slay your precious ones. "Come," they say, "and let us wipe out Israel as a nation—we will destroy the very memory of her existence." This was their unanimous decision at their summit conference—they signed a treaty to ally themselves against Almighty God— these Ishmaelites and Edomites and Moabites and Hagrites; people from the lands of Gebal, Ammon, Amalek, Philistia and Tyre; Assyria has joined them too, and is allied with the descendants of Lot (TLB)

'They are full of craftiness and plot against your people' says verse 3. The crafty plot in Hebrew is *aram sod*. The first word means crafty or shrewd, and the second one expresses the meeting of a company of persons who do something in secret.[216] 'Come', they say, 'let us wipe out Israel as a nation – we will destroy the memory of her existence' says verse 4. This is what the Nazi government did when they conferred in Berlin-Wannsee on the day of 20th January 1942 in order to ensure the collaboration of the heads of the represented government departments in systematically deporting Jews to occupied Poland to kill them. 'Let us destroy them as a nation, so that Israel's name is remembered no more.' This is what the Nazis called the 'final solution to the Jewish question.'

'Assyria has joined them too, and is allied with the descendants of Lot',[217] as recorded in verse eight. The Hebrew word translated 'allied' here is *zeroa*. It means to bring political and military forces against someone. Did you know that 'Assyria' joined the Nazis in the Holocaust? Haj Amin al-Husseini (1895-1974), leader of Arab Palestine during the British Mandate period, and Grand Mufti of Jerusalem, met with Adolf Hitler on the day of 28th November 1941 and collaborated with the Nazis to bring political and military forces against the Jews in Europe and to hinder Jews from entering Palestine. He continued his anti-Jewish influence in the Middle East after World War II. We can see how significantly this Psalm prophesies about events in the last century.

But Restoration for Israel will come from Jesus. Psalm 80:17-18 says, 'Let your hand rest on the man at your right hand, the son of man you have raised up for yourself. Then we will not turn away from you; revive us, and we will call on your name.' The man at God's right hand is Jesus as we have already seen when we looked at Psalm 110. Psalm 80 does not only speak prophetically about destruction and restoration, which Israel saw several times in its history, but also about the final salvation of Israel which Paul wrote about in Romans 11:12, 15 and 25-32. Paul called Israel's salvation 'life from the dead' in verse 15 of his letter.

I would like to look at one more prophecy full of figures of speech, which also points to the Holocaust. It is Psalm 102:1-12. Please read it. When I read 'my days disappear like smoke' (verse 3), 'I am reduced to skin and bones because of all my groaning and despair' (verse 5) or 'I eat ashes instead of bread' (verse 9), I clearly see when these figures of speech became reality in the concentration camps.

Important keys in Scripture regarding writing:

'When the LORD finished speaking to Moses on Mount Sinai, he gave him the two tablets of the covenant law, the

tablets of stone inscribed by the finger of God' (Exodus 31:18).

The messianic psalms: Psalm 2, Psalm 22, and Psalm 110.

'My heart is stirred by a noble theme as I recite my verses for the king; my tongue is the pen of a skillful writer' (Psalm 45:1).

'Therefore every scribe who has become a disciple in the kingdom of heaven is like a head of a household, who brings forth out of his treasure things new and old.' (Matthew 13:52)

Chapter Twelve: Prophetic Action

Outline

When we call a word, a sign, an act or any other creative expression prophetic, we are talking about bringing forth a message from God, speaking about an event in the future or 'drawing heaven to earth' (Matthew 6:10). We have already seen that a prophecy can take many creative forms. Reflecting on what I said in the last chapter about prophetic writing, we know that the Old Testament is full of prophecy. If we specifically look into the Prophets, we see that one creative prophetic expression is recorded over and over again are prophetic acts. For an overview of prophetic acts see appendix 4.

Prophetic acts have two ingredients, a directive or mandate from God to act out or perform an action and the prophetic meaning of the action or performance. The prophetic expression here is action. These actions or performances were often multi-sensory. Look into Ezekiel chapter 4 where the prophet is told to engrave the city of Jerusalem on a clay tile; to lay siege to it; to lie on his left side for 390 days; and then to lie on his right side for 40 days; to be tied up with ropes; to eat set amounts of food and drink set amounts of water; and to cook his food over animal dung. Multi-sensory? Certainly.

Prophetic acts can have distinct functions or results. These can be warfare or victory, as in Aaron and Hur holding up Moses' arms in Exodus 17:10-13; intercession, as the birthing position of Elijah in I Kings 18:42-44; healing, as the seven immersions of Naaman in the Jordan in II Kings 5:9-14; foretelling, as the prophecy of the exile in Ezekiel 4 and 5 or of Paul being turned over to the Romans in Acts 21:10-12; or calling into ministry, as Elijah throwing his coat over

Elisha's shoulders in I Kings 19:19.[218]

Prophetic acts might be witnessed by an audience, but this is not a necessary constituent. If an audience is present, they will be impacted by the action or performance. The question that arises, of course, is, in what way prophetic acts can be considered prophetic art? There is a vigorous debate about this question with prophetic artists settled properly in both camps. I understand artists who arrive at the conclusion that a prophetic act can be prophetic art and I understand artists who believe the opposite. What I am going to write in this chapter is not fact or creed, but a comment on how these actions or performances can be interpreted. To answer this question, we need to look into the nature of the performance or act. Depending on how we qualify the nature of the prophetic act, we can find parallels to several categories of art. We can compare prophetic acts to theatre, or to performance art.

Prophecy as Theatre

Plainly speaking, when I read a prophecy like Ezekiel 12, where the prophet digs through a wall, I can immediately see a dramatic performance. One function of theatre, which was exemplified by Euripides, the tragedian of classical Athens, (c. 480 – c. 406 BC) is that it should reveal reality even if this revelation would not fit the ethical or moral customs, or the conventions of the day. In this way, theatre is an unmasking exercise. It is an action which 'occurs when one or more human beings isolated in time and space present themselves in imagined acts to another or others.'[219] I would follow this definition of theatre, with the exception that the Old Testament prophets were not isolated in space and time performing in front of an audience but usually acted out their prophecies in the midst of the people. Thus, they had an audience, and were not isolated but instead integrated.

A prophetic act is often performed so that an underlying reality is not only revealed but also understood. The audience can only achieve this understanding if they recognize the components of the performance. This means there needs to be an agreed code of actions or symbols between the prophet and the crowd. We can assume that this was the case as most of the prophets used everyday items and situations to reveal underlying, usually spiritual realities. For instance, both Isaiah (29:16) and Jeremiah (18:3-4) used clay and potters to illuminate their messages. Often the message would also be explained, as it was, in Ezekiel 12:10 where God Himself tells the prophet to explain his actions to the people. In order to understand a prophetic act in terms of theatre, we need to see that the dramatist is God, not the prophet. The underlying spiritual reality to be revealed comes from Him.

It is time for a word of caution. If we look at the prophetic acts in the Bible we need to realize that we are looking into a culture separated from us by between 2,000 and 2,800 years. We would not go to a potter's studio today in order to be in an everyday environment for our prophetic performance. We would perhaps go to a mall or a department store to achieve the same effect. When we interpret the prophets' actions as art, we need a serious level of abstraction to apply theatre theory to them.

Prophecy as Performance Art

As prophetic acts are characterized by actions or performances, the connection to performance art seems pretty obvious. Let us look at a modern definition of performance art. It is

> a performance presented to an audience within a fine art context, traditionally interdisciplinary. Performance may be either scripted or unscripted, random or carefully orchestrated, spontaneous or otherwise carefully planned with or without audience participation. … It can be any situation which involves four basic elements: time, space, the performer's body… and a relationship between performer and audience.[220]

We can already see parallels between performance art and prophecy as performance. A performance, presented to an audience, is interdisciplinary, carefully orchestrated, involving time, space, the performer himself and a relationship with the audience. The two differ from each other in that a prophetic act does not occur in a fine art context and can be captured, ie written down so that 'whoever reads it may run with it' (Habakkuk 2:2), whereas performance art is not necessarily presented to be recorded. What they both have in common is that neither has entertainment purposes, but quite the opposite!

Let us now turn to some prophetic acts to see how they can be interpreted as prophetic art.

Creation

Please read Genesis 1. God used His voice to *speak* creation into being. Performance art? Big time! It was a performance, it was interdisciplinary and I can see painting, sculpting, dance and music in the process of creation. It was carefully orchestrated and planned and involved four elements: time ('in the beginning'), the performer (God), space ('the heaven and the earth') and a relationship with the audience ('God created mankind in his own image, in the image of God He created them; male and female He created them'). A dramatic performance? Amazing drama! It revealed reality as God spoke something into being, the earthly realm, which had existed in His mind and heart beforehand, the spiritual realm. God revealed His own character, and His own being in this new physical reality. It comes from Him and has no other source. It is filled with imagination. I cannot think of anything more dramatic than creation appearing out of nothing as God speaks.

Let us examine the action words used in Genesis 1. This extensive list includes to create, to move, to divide, to call, to say, to make, to gather, to appear, to bring forth, to yield, to give light, to rule, to set, to fly, to bless, to be fruitful, to multiply, to fill, to have dominion, to replenish, to subdue, to give and to bear. Wow! Lots of activity and life. Some of these verbs have connotations which further enlighten us to the fact that creation was an interdisciplinary, dramatic performance.

'To move' in verse 2 is the Hebrew word *rachaph*. It is also translated as to hover, to flutter, to tremble (Jeremiah 23:9, NAS) and to shake (Jeremiah 23:9, KJV).[221] 'To call' in verse 5 is the Hebrew word *qara*. It is also translated as to name, to proclaim (Genesis 41:43, NAS); to summon (Genesis 49:1, NAS); to invite (Exodus 2:20, NAS); to offer (Deuteronomy 20:10, NAS); and, to publish (Deuteronomy

32:3, KJV).[222] 'To appear' in verse 9 is the Hebrew word *raah*. It is also translated as to see, to look, to become visible (Genesis 8:5, NAS); to show, to remain alive (Genesis 16:13, NAS); to encounter (Genesis 20:10, NAS); to provide (Genesis 22:8, KJV); to visit (Genesis 34:1, NAS); to supervise (Genesis 39:23, NAS); and, to observe (Genesis 40:6,NAS).[223]

'To yield' in verse 11 in Hebrew is *zara*. It is also translated as to sow (Genesis 26:12, KJV); to give birth (Leviticus 12:2, NAS); to conceive (Numbers 5:28, NAS); to plant (Isaiah 28:24, NAS); to perpetuate (Nahum 1:4, NAS); and, to scatter (Zechariah 10:9, NAS).[224] 'To yield' in verse 12 is the Hebrew term *yatsa*. It is also translated as to flow (Genesis 2:10, NAS); to go out (Genesis 4:16, KJV); to fly (Genesis 8:7, NAS); to depart (Genesis 12:4, KJV); to rise (Genesis 19:23, KJV); to proceed (Genesis 24:50, KJV); and, to leave (Genesis 31:13,NAS).[225]

'To set' in verse 17 is the Hebrew *nathan*. It is also translated as to place, to give, to yield (Genesis 4:12, NAS); to deliver (Genesis 9:2, KJV); to establish (Genesis 17:2, NAS); to commit (Genesis 39:8, KJV); to grant (Genesis 43:14, NAS); to permit (Exodus 3:19, NAS); to allow (Exodus 12:23, NAS); and, to appoint (Exodus 21:23, NAS).[226]

'To fill' in verse 22 is the Hebrew word *male* or *mala*. It is also translated as to replenish (Genesis 1:28, NAS); to complete (Genesis 29:27, NAS); to be satisfied (Exodus 15:9, KJV); to endow (Exodus 28:3, NAS); to ordain (Exodus 28:41, NAS); to consecrate (Exodus 28:41, KJV) to dedicate (Exodus 32:29, NAS); to overflow (Joshua 3:15, KJV) to be armed (II Samuel 23:7, NAS); to confirm (I Kings 1:14, KJV); to accomplish (Esther 2:12, KJV); and, to gather (Job 16:10, KJV).

Now try to paint a painting, write a song or poem, choreograph a dance, create a sculpture or fashion a dress which encompasses most of these action verbs! A challenge? Creation was prophetic performance art and prophetic theatre in which God imagined, constituted, designed, organized, fashioned, composed and gave birth to our reality and the way we understand it.

Passover and Communion

We find the story of Passover in Exodus 12:1-30. Today, Passover is one of the three major Jewish holidays – the other two being *Shavuot* (Feast of Weeks or Pentecost) and *Sukkot* (Feast of Tabernacles). In Exodus 13:3, Moses tells the Israelites to commemorate the day as they are freed from slavery in Egypt. He then goes on in verse six to talk about the seven days of celebrating Passover. On the last day, when a festival is celebrated to the Lord, Moses instructs the Jews to tell their sons: 'I do this because of what the Lord did for me when I came out of Egypt.' Today this verse is quoted four times during the Passover Seder[227] as the Haggadah is read, the Jewish text which sets forth the order of the Seder celebration.

The fact that the verse says 'when *I* came out of Egypt' means that the one celebrating the feast is compelled to consider himself to have come out of Egypt. In other words, those who celebrate the feast are invited to experience the change from slavery to freedom for themselves. This is the point where the feast becomes prophetic. Before the Passover even occurs, the Israelites were told to commemorate the event and to celebrate it in a specific form. They were told to remember and to observe the occasion in Exodus 12:14, 17, 25, 26 and 13:3, 5, 8 and 14. After this, the Passover actually happened and they left Egypt.[228] The fact that they were told that something which had not happened will be celebrated 'year after year' (Exodus 13:10) makes it a prophetic feast. It signifies not only that this feast is an eternal ordinance but also that it was given to be commemorated forever, before it actually came to pass.

There are specific regulations about the meal (Exodus 12:3-6) and how to eat it (12:8-9). The dress code is also very specific (12:10-11). What is described here are people ready for a journey. It is intriguing to realize that the entire populace left Egypt with the same taste in their mouths – a prophetic foreshadowing of Israel becoming a nation.[229] There are many explanations of the meanings of the rituals and foods which constitute the Seder celebration. You can find an overview in Appendix 5. Today all those who celebrate the Seder commemorate and relive the communion and intimacy of sharing not only the same history, but the same tastes, sounds and rituals. The participants *act out* what happened in the past. They are involved in the dramatic performance. Sound familiar? Passover is not only a prophetic reenactment of the escape from slavery, but a composition of prophetic theatre with intense audience involvement. Pinchas Lapide[230] described the celebration of Passover in his book *The Resurrection of Jesus* as 'permeated by a thirst for, and an immediate expectation of, salvation.'[231] This statement demonstrates that the celebration of Passover embodies not only a commemoration of past liberation or an invitation to experience present liberation, but also a prophetic hope of coming salvation.

If we go through the Haggadah, we will realize that Psalms 113-118, called the 'Hallel,' are sung during the Seder. They are sung together as part of the service in the synagogue on all major Jewish holy days. Not so during the Seder. The first two psalms are sung directly before serving the meal whereas the remaining ones are sung after the meal is finished. This is a telling difference we need to notice. Psalm 113 praises God as He governs world and individual affairs as opposed to Psalm 114, which recalls the Exodus which is celebrated in the Seder meal. The four Psalms sung after the meal explain the purpose of the meal: not only to remember what God did physically, but also what He did and is doing spiritually.

Psalm 116:13 refers us to the 'cup of salvation,' which shows us another spiritual connection to the Last Supper and communion. Psalm 118:22 states 'the stone the builders rejected has become the cornerstone,' a prophetic foreshadowing of Jesus the chief cornerstone (Ephesians 2:19-22). Psalm 118:26a says 'Blessed is he who comes in the name of the Lord.' Jesus speaks to Jerusalem in Matthew 23:39 quoting this verse saying that Jerusalem will not see Him again until it confesses that He is the Messiah. The same verse is shouted by the crowds who went ahead of Jesus and followed Him as He entered Jerusalem on a donkey (Mark 11:9). This verse prophetically foreshadows Jesus as the Messiah. Psalm 115:1 is the sum of what Psalms 115-118 express:

'Not to us, Lord, not to us but to your name be the glory, because of your love and faithfulness.'

God told the Israelites prophetically to celebrate the exodus before it happened. This celebration, which is the new bond service of the Israelites to God instead of their bond service to Egypt (Exodus 12:25-26), is to God's glory! It is a prophetic drama reenacted with intense audience participation year after year. This was the prophetic drama Jesus celebrated with His disciples the night He was betrayed when He instituted the celebration of communion[232]. This celebration occurred during Jesus' final journey to Jerusalem. This journey had a purpose which Jesus knew. 'When the time was come, ... he steadfastly set his face to go to Jerusalem' (Luke 9:51, KJV). Jesus had told His disciples what would happen to Him (Matthew 10:32). His disciples thought that 'the kingdom of God should immediately appear' (Luke 19:11). They most likely thought that this would be an appearance in the physical realm; and Jesus would show Himself as the Messiah who would come to overthrow the occupying forces and bring back independence to the Jews. They would have understood Jesus riding into Jerusalem on a donkey as a further step of putting this train of thought into action as described above. But the kingdom Jesus talked about was 'not of this world' (John 18:36).

The Last Supper was a celebration of Passover in the context of Jesus' final, intentional journey to Jerusalem. The celebration would have followed the instructions given in Exodus 12 and 13. At the main course of the meal, the father, in this case Jesus, gave thanks for the unleavened bread, broke it and gave it to the family members, in this case the disciples. Jesus gave this breaking of bread a new meaning as His body given for us, prophetically speaking of His body's breaking on the cross. After the bread and the lamb were eaten, ie after the supper, Jesus took the third cup, the cup of blessing, and gave it a new meaning, by calling it 'the new covenant in my blood which is poured out for you' (Luke 22:20). He spoke prophetically about the shedding of His blood on the cross for the forgiveness of sins.

Jesus and His disciples performed the prophetic drama of Passover, but He gave it new meaning as He turned the prophetic performance of an ancient event into a prophetic parable of His own death.[233] Paul explains this in I Corinthians 11:26 saying 'For whenever you eat this bread and drink this cup, you proclaim the Lord's death until he comes.' The Greek term translated as proclaim is *katagello*, which means announcing, declaring or publishing something with 'the included idea of celebrating, commending, [or] openly praising.'[234] Do you see the element of performance in this term? Jesus did not explain His coming death on the cross to His disciples with words, as we might do today in our sermons. Through the breaking of the bread and the drinking of the wine, He acted out what was about to happen, involving His disciples, as His audience, in a stirring way. They must have been puzzled and shocked as He did this. 'Eat His body, drink His blood?' The eating of the bread and the drinking of the wine involved them in a prophetic act, and a prophetic performance, which gave them a prophetic experience!

Jesus gives the breaking of the bread and the drinking of the cup, both elements of the Passover drama, a new meaning, by prophesying His death to be a new and the ultimate act or performance of liberation and salvation. Paul consequently portrays this in His statement in I Corinthians 5:7, 'For even Christ our Passover is sacrificed for us' (KJV). Jesus called the cup 'the new covenant in my blood' (Luke 22:20). With this covenant language, He referred to the sprinkling of the blood of the sacrifice onto the altar and on the people in Exodus 24:6-8, where the blood is called 'the blood of the covenant.' This means that Jesus spoke of a new sacrifice, Himself, a new and final liberation from sins and a new covenant in His blood. All of these are to be celebrated. It is important to note that He spoke of these things before they occurred, ie He spoke of them prophetically. This is the same manner in which His Father spoke about the Passover drama to be celebrated before the celebrated events occurred. This parallel shows us again that Jesus turned the performance of a prophetic drama of an ancient event into a prophetic parable.

This thought is also supported by what Luke recorded about when this feast or celebration will finally be fulfilled. Jesus said to His disciples that this celebration will 'find fulfillment in the kingdom of God' (Luke 14:16) when 'the kingdom of God comes' (Luke 14:18). Jesus explained what will happen in this kingdom as 'you may eat and drink at my table in my kingdom' (Luke 14:30a). This referred to the marriage banquet of the lamb and the bride[235]. This is another prophetic connection we need to see when we look at the Last Supper and communion as prophetic dramas and performances.

The Other Pilgrim Feasts

Shavuot, or the Feast of Weeks, is known to Christians by its New Testament name and celebration, Pentecost. In Leviticus 23:15-22, God gave the Feast of Weeks. It is to be celebrated 50 days after the Passover Sabbath, hence the name Pentecost, 'fiftieth' in Greek. The Israelites are called to bring a new offering, *chadash minchah*, to the Lord. This new offering is often interpreted and translated as a grain offering or an offering of the first fruits of the land in that season. *Chadash* means 'new' or 'fresh' and is the term used in the new song which occurs seven times in the Old Testament.[236] The same word is used in the often quoted Isaiah 43:19, 'See I am doing a new thing,' and in the prophecies about the new heavens and the new earth in Isaiah 65:17 and 66:22. This offering was to be brought before it was clear how good a harvest was to be reaped. This means that it was an expression of trust, giving away the first part of the harvest without knowing how much there would be.

In Exodus 34:22, it specifies that the offering is to be a wheat offering. Wheat has two prophetic meanings It is a first fruit of the harvest and speaks prophetically of Jesus as the first fruit to be resurrected (I Corinthians 15:23). In the New Testament, Jesus speaks of His disciples when He refers to wheat in His parables (Matthew 3:11-12, 13:24-30 and Luke 3:16-17). Jonathan Bernis explains that, according to traditional Jewish calculations, the feast of Weeks was given at the time when Israel received the Torah at Mount Sinai which transformed Israel from a group of ten tribes and a 'mixed multitude' (Exodus 12:38, KJV) of people into a nation.[237] At Mount Sinai God separated Israel as a community unto Himself for the world to see who He is.

We can draw a prophetic connection between *Shavuot* in the Old Testament and Pentecost in the New Testament. The coming of the

Spirit at Pentecost was fifty days after Jesus' death on the cross, which was the prophetic counterpart of the Exodus. It is viewed as the birth of the church. As God set apart Israel at Mount Sinai to show Himself to the world through a nation, so Jesus set apart His body as a community to show Himself to the world. Both are called a kingdom of priests (Exodus 19:6 and I Peter 2:9). When God met the Israelites at Mount Sinai, there was thunder and lightning (Exodus 19:16), which is reflected in the 'violent wind' in Acts 2:2. God descended on the mountain in fire (Exodus 19:18). This prophetically foretells the Holy Spirit descending on the disciples in tongues of fire (Acts2:3). In both events, the sound and commotion attracts a crowd (Exodus 19:16-17 and Acts 2:6). In Acts 2:6, the crowd is 'bewildered,' and in Exodus 19:16 the people 'tremble.' The writer of Hebrews explains these parallels and their prophetic meanings in much greater detail in Hebrews 12:18-29. The Israelites came to the Mountain of Fear when Shavuot was given, just as the disciples now come to the Mountain of Joy as they follow Jesus (become wheat) and are joined in the resurrection. Moreover, the fact that the Jews who had come to the celebrations in Jerusalem, and could hear the disciples speak in their own languages (Acts 2:6-11), prophetically foreshadows the fact that 'a great multitude' from 'every nation, tribe, people and language' will stand before the throne of God (Revelation 7:9).

Sukkot or the Feast of Tabernacles has two main meanings. One comes from Exodus 23:16 and 34:22 where it is called the 'Festival of Ingathering.' The Hebrew term translated as ingathering or harvest is only used in these two verses in the Old Testament. This name of the feast alludes to the harvest and prophetically speaks of the harvest of souls at the end of the age (Matthew 13:24-30 and 36-43). The feast of Tabernacles is also connected to the nations coming to Jerusalem to worship the Lord after all the nations fought against Jerusalem, and the Lord has come to reign, read Zechariah 14. The ingathering is to be celebrated joyfully and is to include the fatherless, foreigners and widows (Deuteronomy 16:14). This prophetically predicts what Jesus said about feeding the hungry, giving drink to the thirsty, inviting the stranger in, clothing the naked, looking after the sick and visiting the prisoners (Matthew 25:34-40).

The other meaning for the feast comes from Leviticus 23:33-43, where the reference to the harvest is evident, but the focus is on the fact that the feast is celebrated by living in temporary shelters or booths. The reenactment of this part of the exodus speaks of total dependence on the Lord. The living in booths for seven days and the other regulations of the feast clearly depict a drama, as a story is being retold.

During the time of the second Temple, the Jews celebrated a water libation ceremony every day of the feast. Every morning a priest went to the Pool of Siloam and drew a pitcher of fresh, running, water from it. This was also done on the evening before the Sabbath to keep that day holy through rest. The priest then took the water back to the temple, entering the city through the 'Watergate.'[238] He poured the water out with the wine of the drink offering for the morning sacrifice. After the drink offering, the Hallel (Psalms 113-118) would be sung and the temple music began.[239] The pouring of the wine can be found in the descriptions of the drink offerings in Leviticus 23. The pouring of the water is not in the Pentateuch. It comes from the interpretation of three extra letters found in the Hebrew text of Numbers 29:19, 29 and 33 which are linked to fashion the word *mayim*, meaning water.

The waters of the Pool of Siloam had prophetic significance. In Isaiah 44:3, God promises to 'pour water on the thirsty land, and streams on the dry ground; I will pour out my Spirit on your off-spring, and my blessing on your descendants.' Historically, the kings from David's line had been anointed with the waters of Siloam. As anointing was a symbol for the pouring out of the Holy Spirit on someone, the running, living, waters of Siloam were linked with the pouring out of the Spirit of God on Israel. Isaiah 12 speaks about the day of salvation, which is the day when the Messiah comes to liberate Israel. Verse three says, 'With joy you will draw water from the wells of salvation.' The water drawn from the Pool of Siloam symbolized the Spirit of God being poured out when the Messiah comes. Is this ceremony a dramatic performance? The procession from the temple to the Pool and back, together with the music and dances which went on in the temple after the pouring of the water[240] and the waving of tree branches were considered the chief ceremonies of the feast. Try to imagine the choir of Levites singing six Psalms, Rabbis dancing, the priests marching around the Altar and the people creating a forest of trees with the branches. Quite a dramatic performance!

It was against this background that Jesus went to the festivities in secret, as depicted in John 7. People were whispering during the feast about Jesus' identity (verses 12 and 25-27). Some believed He was the Messiah (Verse 31). Nicodemus was among the crowd (verses 50-51). Even the temple guards who were sent to arrest Him, did not obey their command because they were concerned that He was the Messiah (verses 45-47). On the last day of the feast Jesus 'cried out, saying, "If anyone is thirsty, let him come to Me and drink. He who believes in Me, as the Scripture said, 'From his innermost being will flow rivers of living water.'" (John 7:37-38) The Greek term translated cried is *krazo*, which also means to scream. This was not just a statement with a raised voice. The same term is used in Revelation 10:3 where it says that a mighty angel 'gave a loud shout', descending from heaven. This shout is also described in verse three as 'the roar of a lion', and in verse four as 'When he shouted, the voices of the seven thunders spoke.' It is this type of voice Jesus used when He spoke to the masses on the last day of the feast. Is this not quite a performance?

What He said was also extraordinary: He stated that the expectations of those who are thirsty for the outpouring of the Holy Spirit and the coming of the Messiah were fulfilled in Him. The theme of living water flowing is a repeated topic in Isaiah[241] and alludes to the river from the temple in Ezekiel 47. Jesus shouted at the crowd that what this water in the libation ceremony symbolized was fulfilled in Him there, and at that moment. A dramatic performance? By all means! No more whispering as Jesus gave this clear and dramatic statement like the roar of a lion.

Prophetic Acts Today

A lot has been written on prophetic acts for today. I will leave the discovery of the various opinions to your own inquisitiveness. Suffice it to say, that in the context of this book, an action alone does not create a prophetic act. It has to occur in the framework of a divine command to act it out. Every prophecy comes from the Lord and whether it is to be acted out or communicated in a different way is only a question of delivery. However, it can often be challenging to understand the meaning behind prophetic acts with our natural minds. A prophetic act is often an act of simple obedience, and this can apply to the delivery of all prophecy.

We have sometimes used symbols in prophetic actions. Oil has several meanings and can symbolize anointing (Exodus 29:7, Leviticus 8:30, I Samuel 16:13); joy (Psalm 45:7, Isaiah 61:3, Hebrews 1:8-9); preparation for burial (Mark 14:3-8); healing (Mark 6:13 and James 5:14); being filled with the Spirit (I Samuel 16:13); consecration (Exodus 28:41 and 40:9;) and, unity (Psalm 133:2). Remember that the anointing oil in the tabernacle was a piece of art, 'the work of a perfumer' (Exodus 30:25, NASB). When we talk about symbols used in a prophetic act, please keep in mind, that the action originates from the Lord, and not from the symbol.

About 15 years ago, we had joined with a group of intercessors in front of the parliament building in my home state in Germany to pray for the politicians. Across from this building was a multi-story car park with a massive piece of art on its side. The art celebrated mammon, lust and prostitution. I had brought a bottle of virgin olive oil and one of the other intercessors threw most of the oil all over this monstrosity, as we prayed. It had been there for years. We returned to intercede at the same spot once a month. After a few months had passed, we realized that the art had been dismantled and taken away. A prophetic performance? Yes, of course! Results? The results were overturning, in the literal sense of the word.

Salt can symbolize a covenant with God (Leviticus 2:3) or an everlasting covenant (Numbers 18:19); the inauguration of rulers (II Chronicles 13:4-5); barrenness (Jeremiah 17:5-8 and Ezekiel 47:11); disobedience (Genesis 19:26); purification (II Kings 2:19-22); and, judgement (Mark 9:49). Don't forget that the disciples of Jesus are called the 'salt of the earth' (Matthew 5:13).

Wine, on the other hand, can both be a positive or a negative symbol. It is used negatively to express the wrath of God (Psalm 75:8, Jeremiah 25:15 and Revelation 14:8-10); violence (Proverbs 4:17); delusion (Jeremiah 51:7); and, immorality (Revelation 14:8-10). It is used positively to signify hospitality and peace (Genesis 14:17-18); celebration (Isaiah 25:6 and John 2:1-11, Jesus' first miracle); worship (Exodus 29:40 and Leviticus 23); first fruits (Deuteronomy 18:4-5); abundance (Genesis 27:28, Proverbs 3:9-10 and Joel 3:18); gladness (Psalm 4:7 and Jeremiah 31:12); restoration (Amos 9:13-14); fresh circumstances (Matthew 9:17 and Mark 2:22); and, especially the forgiveness of sins, the new covenant and Jesus' blood (Matthew 26:27-28, Mark 14:23-24, Luke 22:20 and I Corinthians 11:25-26).

Important keys in Scripture regarding prophetic action:

Creation as a prophetic performance: Genesis 1.

Passover and the Last Supper as prophetic dramas in Exodus 12:1-30 and Luke 22:7-23.

Engraving a tile and performing a drama in Ezekiel 4 and 5.

The exile as a prophetic performance in Ezekiel 12.

In the last day, that great day of the feast, Jesus stood and cried, saying, If any man thirst, let him come unto me, and drink. He that believeth on me, as the scripture hath said, out of his belly shall flow rivers of living water (John 7:37-38, KJV).

Endnotes

1   James Strong, Strong's Exhaustive Concordance of the Bible, H430

2   https://www.bible.ca/trinity/trinity-oneness-unity-plural-of-majesty-plura-lis-majestaticus-royal-we.htm, retrieved 9th May 2020.

3   As quoted in: Creativity in the Bible, Part 2, www.worshipinfo.com/creativity-in-the-bible-part-2-of-2, retrieved 15th March 2016.

4   James Strong, Strong's Exhaustive Concordance of the Bible, No. 6754.

5   www.ancient-hebrew.org/40_genesis1.html, retrieved 15th March 2016.

6   As quoted in: http://www.societyofsacredheart.org/spirituality/laughter-and-god?start=1

7   Joseph Ratzinger [Pope Benedict XVI], In the Beginning: A Catholic Understanding of the Story of Creation and the Fall, (Grand Rapids, MI: Eerdmans, 1995), 44-45, 47.

8   James Strong, Strong's Exhaustive Concordance of the Bible, G4160

9   http://alleysonmission.blogspot.com/2015/10/we-are-his-workman-ship-ephesians-210.html, retrieved August 14th, 2019

10   James Strong, Strong's Exhaustive Concordance of the Bible, H8085

11   https://en.wikipedia.org/wiki/Shema_Yisrael, retrieved 25th February 2019

12   These steps are based on the teaching by Donna Jordan about Hearing God's voice and have been adapted, www.ywamkb.net/kb/Hearing_God%27s-Voice, retrieved 26th April 2014

13   James Strong, Strong's Exhaustive Concordance of the Bible, H1927

14   Ibid., H5278

15   C. S. Lewis, The Weight of Glory, New York: HarperCollins, 2001, 42

16   James Strong, Strong's Exhaustive Concordance of the Bible, H6643

17   Ibid., H4758

18 Ibid., H3302

19 Wayne Grudem, Systematic Theology, Leicester/Grand Rapids, 1994, 219

20 Brian Zahnd, Beauty will save the World, Lake Mary: Charisma House, 2012, 45

21 James Strong, Strong's Exhaustive Concordance of the Bible, G827

22 https://enduringword.com/bible-commentary/1-corinthians-1, retrieved 19th September 2019

23 James Strong, Strong's Exhaustive Concordance of the Bible, G3056

24 As quoted in Bob Kauflin, Should We Worship Jesus as the Beautiful One?, http://worshipmatters.com/2007/07/20/qa-friday-shou-2, retrieved 9th May 2017

25 http://grahamkendrick.co.uk/songs/graham-kendrick-songs/magnificent-warrior/come-see-the-beauty-of-the-lord, retrieved 2nd May 2017

26 As quoted in Behind The Song With Kevin Davis, # 195, https://newreleasetoday.com/article.php?article_id=519, retrieved 7th February 2019

27 Ibid.

28 https://www.hep.physik.uni-siegen.de/~grupen/kukokoeln.pdf, page 6, retrieved 15th March 2019

29 Albert Camus, Create Dangerously, Penguin 2018, 21.

30 Joachim Kardinal Meisner, 1933-2017; in his sermon at the opening of the Kolumba Museum in Cologne in 2017; www.welt.de/debatte/kommentare/article6070085/In-der-Schoepfung-dem-Schoepfer-auf-die-Spur-zu-kommen-ist-die-Aufgabe-der -Kuenstler.html, retrieved 15th March 2019

31 Rodolfo Papa, Kunst als Bewahrung der Schönheit der Schöpfung (Erster Teil), published 4th December 2014, https://de.zenit.org/articles/kunst-als-bewahrung-der-schonheit-der-schopfung-erster-teil, retrieved 15th March 2019

32 American author, born 1960

33 Jeremy Begbie, Voicing Creation's Praise: Towards a Theology of the Arts, Edinburgh: Blackwell 1991, 170, 174

34 Title of the conversation between him and Yvon Taillandieron, Miro's life and work, first published in 1954.

35 Robin M. Jensen, The Substance of Things Seen, Art, Faith and the Christian Community, Grand Rapids, 2004, 33

36   With the exceptions of the Christophanies in the Old Testament

37   James Strong, Strong's Exhaustive Concordance of the Bible, G4561

38   Ibid., G4637

39   www.christinapost.com/news/bono-psalms-missing-christian-music-182939, retrieved 16th June 2018

40   https://www.goodreads.com/quotes/75455-he-who-works-with-his-hands-is-a-laborer-he, retrieved 19th March 2019

41   Edith Schaeffer, Hidden Art, London: The Norfolk Press, 1971, 208

42   James Strong, Strong's Exhaustive Concordance of the Bible, H2796

43   Ibid., H4390

44   Christ John Otto, An Army Arising, why Artists are on the Frontline of the next Move of God, Belonging House Creative, 2013, 24

45   This might not be the same geographical place, but I want to point out the connection through the name.

46   James Strong, Strong's Exhaustive Concordance of the Bible, G1063

47   Ibid., H1692

48   Ibid., H7229

49   Ibid., H2233

50   Ibid., G2192

51   Ibid., H6622

52   Ibid., G4483

53   Matt Tommey, Artist, Author and Mentor, http://www.matttommeymentoring.com, Facebook post in 'The Worship Studio' Facebook group on 24th April 2014.

54   James Strong, Strong's Exhaustive Concordance of the Bible, H7121

55   Ibid., H215

56   Ibid., H3034

57   Ibid., H3027

58   Ibid., H4390

59   Ibid., H3634

60   Christ John Otto, Bezalel: Redeeming a Renegade Generation, Belonging House Creative, 2015

61   James Strong, Strong's Exhaustive Concordance of the Bible, H5564

62   Ibid., H5414

63   https://www.goodreads.com/quotes/tag/art, retrieved 8th April 2019

64   James Strong, Strong's Exhaustive Concordance of the Bible, H4234

65   Ibid., H2342

66   https://www.biblestudytools.com/topical-verses/bible-verses-about-dancing,
      retrieved 10th August 2018

67   James Strong, Strong's Exhaustive Concordance of the Bible, G4640

68   Ibid., G20

69   Ibid., H7797

70   Ibid., H1523

71   Ibid., G21

72   Ibid., H7363

73   Ibid., G3738

74   Ibid., G5525

75   Ibid., G5567

76   Ibid., G2947

77   The history of dance in the Church, http://www.refinedundignified.com/the-
      history-of-dance-in-the-church.html, retrieved August 10th, 2018

78   James Strong, Strong's Exhaustive Concordance of the Bible, H5970

79   Ibid., H2287

80   Ibid., H3769

81   Dvora Lapson, The History of Jewish Dance, https://myjewishlearning.com/
      article/all-my-bones-cry-out-to-the-lord, retrieved August 10th, 2018

82   Ibid.

83   James Strong, Strong's Exhaustive Concordance of the Bible, H3381

84   Ibid., H1980

85   Ibid., H935

86   Ibid., H1980

87   Ibid., H6805

88   Ibid., H1523

89   Ibid., H622

90   Ibid., H7270

91   Ibid., G2380

92   Ibid., H117

93   Ibid., H5307

94   She shared this story with me in a private message on May 8th, 2019. I know her from a Facebook group for prophetic artists.

95   She shared her story with me in a private message on May 4th, 2019. I know her from a Facebook group for prophetic artists.

96   Brian Mills shared the story on February 6th, 2008.

97   James Strong, Strong's Exhaustive Concordance of the Bible, H5264

98   Ibid., H1713

99   Based on work by Christa Egli, Glaubenszentrum Bad Gandersheim

100   James Strong, Strong's Exhaustive Concordance of the Bible, H226

101   Ibid., H7893

102   Ibid., H6531

103   Alfred Edersheim, The Temple – Its Ministry And Services, Peabody: Hendrickson Publishers, 1994, 34

104   James Strong, Strong's Exhaustive Concordance of the Bible, H1984

105   Ibid., G5316

106   Ereo, to utter; laleo, to talk, to preach; lego, speak, to set out a discourse, to mean; phemi, to say, to affirm, to make known one's thoughts; rheo, to speak, to pour forth, to break silence

107   James Strong, Strong's Exhaustive Concordance of the Bible, H8085

108   Ibid.,, H1696

109   Ibid., H1300

110   https://www.youtube.com/watch?v=awkO61T6i0k, retrieved May 17th, 2020

111   Raise a Hallelujah, by Jonathan Helser and Melissa Helser, Bethel Music

112   Raise a Hallelujah. Written by Jonathan David Helser, Melissa Helser, Molly Skaggs, and Jake Stevens. © 2018 Bethel Music Publishing (ASCAP) (100%) All Rights Reserved. Used by Permisison

113   Psalm 33:3; Psalm 40:3; Psalm 96:1; Psalm 98:1; Psalm 144:9; Psalm 149:1; Isaiah 42:10; Zephaniah 3:14-17

114   James Strong, Strong's Exhaustive Concordance of the Bible, H2319

115   On Prophetic Worship, https://hannysetiawan.wordpress.com/category/prophetic-worship/page/1, retrieved 11th May 2019

116   It is still there at the beginning of Solomon's reign (see II Chronicles 1:3 and 13)

117   James Strong, Strong's Exhaustive Concordance of the Bible, H1875

118   They were probably veiled.

119   James Strong, Strong's Exhaustive Concordance of the Bible, H5647

120   Ibid., H2388

121   Psalm 132:2

122   II Chronicles 23

123   II Chronicles 29

124   II Chronicles 35

125   Ezra 3:10-13

126   Nehemiah 7:1 and 12:27-46

127   James Strong, Strong's Exhaustive Concordance of the Bible, G3007

128   Karl Vaters, http://newsmallchurch.com/new-music-2, retrieved 2nd October 2019

129   Psalms 3-9, 11-32, 34, 36-41, 51-65, 68-70, 86, 101, 103, 108-109, 122, 129, 131, 133, 138-145

130   Nahum Sarna, Study of representative Psalms

131   James Strong, Strong's Exhaustive Concordance of the Bible, H2167

132   Based on Neil W. Levin, The Book of Psalms and its Musical Interpretations, https://www.milkenarchive.org/articles/view/the-book-of-psalms-and-its-musical-interpretations, retrieved July 10th, 2018

133   Definition by the World Federation of Music Therapists, taken from: Christian Music Therapy, A Clinical Perspective, https://www.wfmt.info/, retrieved 30th September 2019

134   James Strong, Strong's Exhaustive Concordance of the Bible, H7304

135   Aluede, C. O., and D. B. Ekewenu, Healing Through Music and Dance in the Bible: Its Scope, Competence and Implications for the Nigerian Music Healers, in: Ethno-Med, 3(2), 159-163 (2009)

136   James Strong, Strong's Exhaustive Concordance of the Bible, H6446

137 Ibid., H2707

138 Ibid., H8504

139 Ibid., H3758

140 Ibid., H8144

141 Ibid., H119

142 Ibid., H711

143 Ibid., H8438

144 Exodus 16:20; Deuteronomy 28:39; Job 25:6; Psalm 22:6; Isaiah 14:11, 14, 66:24; and Jonah 4:7

145 James Strong, Strong's Exhaustive Concordance of the Bible, H8320

146 Ibid., H3835

147 Ibid., H2742a

148 Ibid., H3700

149 Ibid., G2847

150 Ibid., G4442

151 Ibid., G3022

152 Ibid., H4886

153 Ute Horn, Als das Leben stehen blieb. Meine Erfahrungen an der Schwelle des Todes, Holzgerlingen: SCM, 2015, pp. 137-138

154 Richard Viladesau, as quoted in: Martin, Chad, Visual Images as Text? Toward a Mennonite Theology of the Arts, https://uwaterloo.ca/grebel/publications/conrad-grebel-review/issues/fall-2005/visual-images-text-toward-mennonite-theology-arts, retrieved 14th January 2019

155 Libreria Editrice Vaticana, Address of His Holiness Benedict XVI, 21st November 2009, http://w2.vatican.va/content/benedict-xvi/en/speeches/2009/november/documents/hf_ben-xvi_spe_20091121_artisti.html, retrieved December 29th, 2018

156 Ibid.

157 Ibid.

158 Sandro Magister, A Catechism for the Culture of the Image, http://chiesa.espresso.repubblica.it/articulo/35203?eng=y, retrieved May 23rd, 2015

159 Ibid.

160   Verdon, Timothy, "New" art in service of the Word, as quoted in: Magister, Sandro, The Pro's and Con's of the New Liturgical Lectionary. Two Experts Go Head to Head, http://fisheaters.com/forums/index.php?topic=2540902.0, retrieved August 14th, 2015

161   Ibid.

162   James Strong, Strong's Exhaustive Concordance of the Bible, H6459

163   Ibid., H6754

164   Ibid., H4327

165   Ibid., H4639

166   Exodus 26:36, 27:16, 28:39, 36:37, 38:18, and 39:29

167   Exodus 27:4 and 38:4

168   Exodus 30:25, 30:35, and II Chronicles 16:14

169   James Strong, Strong's Exhaustive Concordance of the Bible, H8394

170   Ibid., H4395

171   Ibid., H7049

172   I Kings 6:29, 32, 35

173   Judges 20:16, I Samuel 17:49, 25:29, and Jeremiah 10:18

174   James Strong, Strong's Exhaustive Concordance of the Bible, H8313

175   Possibly a shoemaker or tailor

176   Spurgeon, C. H., Autobiography, The Early Years 1, 87-88, as quoted in: Piper, John, The Son of Man Must Be Lifted Up – Like the Serpent, https://www.desiringgod.org/messages/the-son-of-man-must-be-lifted-up-like-the-serpent, retrieved August 4th, 2018

177   James Strong, Strong's Exhaustive Concordance of the Bible, H2025

178   Ibid., G1041

179   Ibid., H8354

180   We see the same story in Deuteronomy 27:1-8

181   Jacob goes there a second time in Genesis 35:1-15

182   James Strong, Strong's Exhaustive Concordance of the Bible, G5097

183   Ibid., H3334

184   The other translations are mortar, heaps, mire, or homer. The latter is a measuring unit which equals about 220 litres.

185 James Strong, Strong's Exhaustive Concordance of the Bible, H2560

186 II Corinthians 6:16

187 This refers back to Leviticus 26:12, Jeremiah 32:38 and Ezekiel 37:27

188 Matthew 27:32-33, Mark 15:22 and Hebrews 13:12

189 James Strong, Strong's Exhaustive Concordance of the Bible, H6440

190 https://en.wikipedia.org/wiki/Installation_art, retrieved August 15th, 2019

191 Ibid.

192 Ibid.

193 He reigned from 69AD to 79AD.

194 James Strong, Strong's Exhaustive Concordance of the Bible, H7069

195 Isaiah 11:2-3; Revelation 1:4; 3:1; 4:5; 5:6

196 He was born around 550BC and reigned Persia from 522BC to 486BC.

197 We find the story in I and II Maccabees, which are book included in the Septuagint and in Old Testament versions of the Catholic and Orthodox churches where they are deemed deuterocanonical.

198 James Strong, Strong's Exhaustive Concordance of the Bible, G4137

199 Ibid., H3722

200 Psalm 56:9, 69:28, 87:6, 139:16, Daniel 12:1, Malachi 3:16, Luke 10:20, Philippians 4:3, Revelation 3:5, 13:8, 17:8, 20:12, 15, 21:27

201 https://bible.org/seriespages/scribes, retrieved September 2nd, 2018

202 http://www.jewishencycolpedia.com/articles/13356-scribes, retrieved September 9th, 2018

203 https://vision.org.au/radio/2018/10/24/bible-jewish-scribes-dead-sea-scrolls/, retrieved September 3rd, 2019

204 His descend from Aaron is spelt out in Ezra 7:1-5

205 The parables of the sower, of the weeds, of mustard and leaven, of the hidden treasure, of the pearl of great value, of the net and of the new and old treasure

206 Matthew 6:21

207 James Strong, Strong's Exhaustive Concordance of the Bible, H3956

208 Isaiah 16:5

209 https://bible.org/seriespage/5-poetical-books, retrieved 19th July 2018

210   These distinctions are based on: http://angelfire.com/sc3/we_dig_montana/
Poetryp2.hyml, retrieved 12th July 2018

211   We find alliteration, anadiplosis, anthropomorphisms, epanalepsis, hyperboles,
implications, metaphors, metonymies, paronomasias, personification, pleo-
nasms, rhetorical questions, similes and zoomorphisms.

212   James Strong, Strong's Exhaustive Concordance of the Bible, H3205

213   John 1:14, 18, 3:16, 18, I John 4:9, 5:1 and 18

214   Matthew 22:44, 26:64, Mark 14:62, 16:19, Luke 20:42, 22:69, Acts 2:33-34,
5:31, 7:55-56, Romans 8:34, Ephesians 1:20, Colossians 3:1, Hebrews 1:3, 13,
8:1, 10:12-13, 12:2, I Peter 3:22

215   James Strong, Strong's Exhaustive Concordance of the Bible, H4066

216   Ibid., H5472

217   According to Genesis 19:36-38 the descendants of Lot were the Moabites and
the Ammonites.

218   These examples are taken from Helen Calder, The Power of a Prophetic Act,
https://www.enlivenpublishing.com/blog/2010/6/29/the-power-of-a-pro-
phetic-act, retrieved 29th May 2019

219   Bernhard Beckerman, Dynamics of Drama, New York: Drama Book
Specialists, 1979, 20

220   Performance Art, https://wikipedia.org/wiki/Performance_art, retrieved 11th
August 2019

221   James Strong, Strong's Exhaustive Concordance of the Bible, H7363

222   Ibid., H7121

223   Ibid., H7200

224   Ibid., H2232

225   Ibid., H3318

226   Ibid., H5414

227   The ritual feast which marks the beginning of Passover

228   Exodus 12:37 and then 13:17

229   Israel became a nation when she received the ten commandments at Mount
Sinai.

230   Jewish theologian and Israeli historian, born 1922, died 1997. My mother read
his books when I was a teenager.

231   London: SPCK, 1984, p. 70

232   Matthew 26:20-29, Mark 14:17-25, Luke 22:14-38, John 13:1-30

233   See: https://biblicalstudies.org.uk/article_supper_dwenham.html, retrieved 3rd June 2019

234   https://www.blueletterbible.org/lang/lexicon/lexicon.cfm?t=k-jv&strongs=G2605, retrieved 24th September 2019.

235   Exodus 24:11, Isaiah 25:6, Matthew 22:1-14, Luke 14:15-24, Revelation 3:20 and 19:7-9

236   Psalm 33:3, 40:3, 96:1, 98:1, 144:9, 149:1 and Isaiah 42:10

237   https://mjbi.org/2012/05/01/shavuot-rich-prophetic-significance, retrieved Biblical Foundations of Prophetic Art - 4.indd 176 26/07/2020 17:02 Endnotes 177 3rd June 2019

238   It was at this gate that Ezra read the law to the people and they rediscovered the feast of Tabernacles and celebrateed it (Nehemiah 8).

239   These facts are taken from Alfred Edersheim, The Temple – Its Ministry And Services, Peabody: Hendrickson Publishers Inc., 1994, pp 220-221

240   Ibid.

Appendix 1 — Movements in prophetic dance, their meanings and corresponding Bible verses

Movement	Meaning	Original Words and Reference
Bowing	Worship, reverence	*naphal* – Genesis 17:2 and Ruth 2:10 *shachah* – Genesis 18:2, 33:3 & Isaiah 66:23 *qadad* – Exodus 4:31, 12:27 & II Chronicles 20:18 *kara* – Psalm 95:6 *pipto* – Matthew 2:11 *klino* – Luke 24:5 *kampto* – Philippians 2:10
Bowing the head or slumping over	Shame, guilt	*shachah* – Psalm 38:6 *kaphaph* – Psalm 146:8 *yarad* – Lamentations 2:10
Clapping hands	Excitement, happiness, joy	*taqa* – Psalm 47:1 *macha* – Psalm 98:8 & Isaiah 55:12
Contractions	Pain	*chiyl* – Psalm 48:6 *tsiyr* – Isaiah 13:6 & 21:3 *tsarar* – Jeremiah 49:2 *thlipsis* – John 16:21
Falling, collapsing	Weakness	*kashal* – Psalm 107:12 *naphal* – Psalm 145:14 & Ecclesiastes 4:10 *kataballo* – II Corinthians 4:9

Movement	Meaning	Original Words and Reference
Isolated movements	Lack of freedom, bondage	*asiyr* – Psalm 107:10 *gadar* – Lamentations 3:7 *desmeo* – Luke 8:29
Kneeling	Humility	*barak/berak* – Psalm 95:6 & Daniel 6:10 *gonupeteo* – Mark 10:17 *tithemi gonu* – Luke 22:41 *gonu kampto* – Romans 14:11 & Philippians 2:10
Leaping, jumping	Joy, triumph, victory	*pazaz* – II Samuel 6:16 *dalag* – Isaiah 35:6 *exallomai* – Acts 3:8 *skirtao* – Luke 1:41 and 44
Lifting arms or hands	Surrender	*paras* – I Kings 8:22 *moal* – Nehemiah 8:6 *nasa* – Psalm 28:2 and 119:48 *naseth* – Psalm 141:2
Muscle arms, fist	Strength, power, might	*natah zeroa* – Deuteronomy 9:29 *nachath zeroa* – II Samuel 22:35 & Psalm 18:34 *zeroa ale* – Job 40:9 *chophen* – Proverbs 30:4 *amats zeroa* – Proverbs 31:17

Appendix 2 — Prophetic Meaning of Colours

These meanings are not intended to be taken as doctrine but are offered as interpretations which can be derived from the respective Bible references. If the colour is only mentioned in a certain translation of the Word, the translation is indicated below.

Amber	God's glory and his bright presence (Ezekiel 1:4; 1:27–28; 8:2 — KJV)
Black	Beauty (Song of Songs 5:11)
Blue	God's Presence (Numbers 4:7, 9, 11)
	God's Throne (Ezekiel 1:26; 10:1)
	Heaven (Exodus 24:10)
	Priestly Garments (Exodus 28:31 — possibly violet)
	Royal Garments (Esther 8:15)
	The Commandments of the Lord (Numbers 15:38–40 possibly violet)
	The Holy Spirit (John 4:13–14; 7:37–39; Revelation 22:17)
	Water
Brown	Soil, Humankind (Genesis 2:7)
Copper	Forgiveness, Righteousness, Sacrifice (Exodus 27:1–2)
Emerald	God's Presence (Revelation 4:3)
Gold	Holy (Exodus 28:36)
	Purification (Revelation 3:18)
	Testing (Zechariah 13:9 and Job 23:10)
	Victory (Revelation 4:4)

Green   Firstfruits (Leviticus 2:14)
             Fruitfulness (Jeremiah 17:8)
             Life (Psalm 92:14)
             Prosperity (Proverbs 11:28)
             Provision (Genesis 1:30; Job 39:8)
             Rest (Psalm 23:2)
             Tenderness (II Kings 19:26)
             Trust (Psalm 52:8)

Grey   Beauty (Proverbs 20:29 — of old age)
             Honour, Respect (Leviticus 19:32)
             Mourning (Esther 4:3 — by association with ashes)
             Repentance (Job 42:6; Matthew 11:21 — by association
             with ashes)

Indigo   Atonement (Numbers 4:6 — the covering of the outer
             Tabernacle)

Orange   Fire (Exodus 3:2)
             God's Voice (Exodus 3:2)

Pink   Healing (a combination of purity [white] and salvation
             [red])

Purple   Riches (Luke 16:19)
             Royalty (Judges 8:26; Esther 8:15)

Red   Blood (Deuteronomy 12:23)
             Cleansing (Leviticus 14:4, 52 — also scarlet or crimson)
             Covenant (Exodus 24:8; Matthew 26:28)
             Forgiveness (Hebrews 9:22)
             Life (Deuteronomy 12:23)
             Passover (Exodus 12:13)
             Redemption (Hebrews 9:12)
             Sacrifice (Exodus 23:18)
             Salvation (Exodus 12:13; Joshua 2:17–21; Romans 5:9)
             Sin (Isaiah 1:18 — also scarlet or crimson)
             The Word of God (Revelation 9:13)

Silver   Refinement (Zechariah 13:9)

White   Angels (John 20:10; Acts 1:10)
               Glory of God (Mark 9:3; Matthew 17:2; Luke 9:29)
               Holiness, Purity, Righteousness (Psalm 51:7; Isaiah 1:18;
               Daniel 7:9; 12:10; Revelation 3:4–5; 7:9; 7:14)
               Victory (Revelation 9:14)

Yellow   Great Value (Psalm 68:13)

Appendix 3 — Codifications for the copying of the Law

Before starting to write

Only clean animal skins could be used to write on and to bind the manuscripts.

A specific and dedicated black ink was to be used.

Each text column only permitted for 48-60 lines.

Only a certain number of letters and words was permitted per page.

If any mistake was made or found on a page, the page was condemned. Three mistakes condemned the whole manuscript.

If two letters touched each other, the document became invalid.

The manuscripts could only be stored in sacred places like synagogues.

As it was forbidden to throw away writings containing the name of God, worn-out scrolls would be temporarily stored in a genizah, a storage place in a synagogue or cemetery, before being buried in a cemetery.

During the copying

Each word was read alone and aloud from an authentic copy before it was written to ensure accuracy.

When the word God was to be written the scribe's pen had to be cleaned.

When the word YHWH was to be written, the scribe had to wash his body before writing it.

Each letter and word had a certain distance from each other. They were not allowed to touch each other.

The lines had to be traced and squared so that the writing was straight and uniform.

After the writing

A review was to be done within 30 days of finishing the manuscript.

Each letter and word was counted.

Each page was rigorously checked; words and letters were counted; and, the beginning, mid-point and final letters were all identified.

Appendix 4 — Prophetic Acts or Dramas

This is only a selection of important prophetic acts in Scripture

Scripture Reference	Acts or Dramas	Interpretation
Genesis 1–2	Creation	Creation is a prophetic drama and performance in which God brings everything into being by speaking it.
Exodus 7:8–13	Aaron's staff becomes a serpent and eats the staffs of Pharaoh's magicians.	Egypt will be defeated by the Lord.
Exodus 12:1–13	Passover	Passover is a prophetic performance with symbolic rituals and foods.
Exodus 23:16 and 34:22 and Leviticus 23:33–43	Sukkot or the Feast of Tabernacles	It prophetically speaks of the harvest of souls, utter dependence on God and of Jesus as the living water.

Scripture Reference	Acts or Dramas	Interpretation
Leviticus 23:15–22	Shavuot or the Feast of Weeks	It speaks of Jesus as the first fruit to be resurrected and of the harvest of souls. It foreshadows the prophetic drama of Pentecost and the outpouring of the Holy Spirit.
I Kings 11:29–39	Ahijah tears a new cloak into 12 pieces and gives ten pieces to King Jeroboam of Israel.	The kingdom will be divided: ten tribes will form the kingdom of Israel while two will form the kingdom of Judah.
II Kings 13:14–17	King Jehoash of Israel shoots arrows at the command of Elisha.	The King will destroy the Arameans completely.
II Kings 13:18–19	King Jehoash of Israel strikes the ground three times with arrows at the command of Elisha.	Because he stopped at three strikes, the King will only defeat Aram three times.
Isaiah 5:1–7	The story of God's vineyard These verses are a prophetic song!	The vineyard of the Lord is the house of Israel and the men of Judah are His pleasant plant (verse 7).

Scripture Reference	Acts or Dramas	Interpretation
Isaiah 5:1–7 (*continued*)	God planted a vineyard in a fruitful hill.	God chose the land of Canaan as the land flowing with 'milk and honey' for His people to dwell.
	He dug it up and cleared out its stones.	God had Israel conquer the land and removed the detestable sin of the land.
	God planted the choicest vine.	Israel is often called the chosen vine. It was established in the land.
	God build a tower [a watch tower] in the middle.	God gave the law to Israel and made a covenant with her. He gave the prophets and protected her from her enemies.
	God made a winepress in it to harvest the good grapes.	The winepress is a symbol of obedience and judgement. Israel was to be the model nation leading the nations into the kingdom of God in the harvest of souls.

Scripture Reference	Acts or Dramas	Interpretation
Isaiah 20:1–4	Isaiah walks about naked for three years.	God said that the king of Assyria will lead away the Egyptians as prisoners and the Ethiopians as captives in the same manner.
Jeremiah 13:1–11	Jeremiah puts a linen belt around his waist.	The belt symbolizes the people's original closeness to the Lord.
	Jeremiah goes to the Euphrates and hides the belt in a hole in the rock.	The people refuse to hear God's words, they walk in the stubbornness of their hearts and walk after other gods to serve and worship them (verse 10).
	Jeremiah dugs up the belt again and it is ruined, good for nothing.	The people lost the connection with God and are good for nothing.
Jeremiah 19:1–13	Jeremiah goes to the Valley of the Son of Hinnom with some of the elders of the people and of the priests.	Hinnom was the valley where some of the Kings of Judah sacrificed their children by fire (verses 4 and 5). It was considered cursed and a symbol for hell.

Scripture Reference	Acts or Dramas	Interpretation
Jeremiah 19:1–13 (*continued*)	Jeremiah breaks an earthen vessel in front of the men. It is impossible to put it back together again.	In the same manner God will destroy the people and the city because of their sin, and bury them in that valley.
Jeremiah 27	Jeremiah makes bonds and yokes and puts them on their neck. Then he sends them to the king of Edom, the king of Moab, the king of the Ammonites, the king of Tyre and the king of Sidon.	All these lands will be given to Nebuchadnezzar king of Babylon.
	He also speaks in a similar manner to Zedekiah King of Judah.	King Zedekiah is challenged to come under submission to the king of Babylon a he is God's tool of judgement.
Jeremiah 51:59–64	Jeremiah sends a scroll to Babylon with Seraiah the staff officer. Seraiah throws the scroll into the Euphrates.	As the scroll sinks into the river so Babylon will sink to rise no more.

Scripture Reference	Acts or Dramas	Interpretation
Ezekiel 4:1–3	Ezekiel draws the outline of Jerusalem on a tile and lays siege to it.	Jerusalem will be besieged and fall because of her sin.
Ezekiel 4:4–8	Ezekiel lies on his left side for 390 days and then on his right side for 40 days, tied up with ropes.	The times signify the amounts of years Israel (390) and Judah (40) have sinned against the Lord.
Ezekiel 4:9–11 and 16–17	Ezekiel is to eat certain amounts of food and drink certain amounts of water.	Food and water will be scarce and they will eat rationed food in anxiety and rationed water in despair.
Ezekiel 4:12–15	Ezekiel is to bake his food over human excrement.	This is a symbol of how deeply the people have defiled themselves.
Ezekiel 5:1	Ezekiel is to shave his head and beard.	A symbol of shame.
Ezekiel 5:2–12	Ezekiel is to burn a third of his hair, to strike a third with the sword and to scatter a third to the wind.	God will punish Jerusalem. A fire will spread from Jerusalem to all Israel. God will pursue her with the sword. A third will die of the plague or perish of famine, a third will fall by the sword and a third will be scattered to the winds.

Scripture Reference	Acts or Dramas	Interpretation
Ezekiel 12:1–16	Ezekiel packs his belongings, digs through a wall and takes his belonging out through it. He covers his eyes as he leaves so that he cannot see the land.	He symbolizes the exile. In like fashion the Israelites will go. Their prince will put his belongings on his shoulder, a hole will be dug through a wall for him and he will go out through it. He will cover his face and not see the land.
Ezekiel 12:17–20	Ezekiel is to tremble as he eats his food and to shake as he drinks his water.	The Israelites will eat their food in anxiety and drink their water in despair because of the violence that will come.
Ezekiel 24:1–13	Ezekiel put choice pieces of meat in a cooking pot and cooks them. He piles on the wood and makes the pot so hot that the bones of the meat get charred and the pot gets glowing hot.	God tried to correct Israel, but all efforts failed. Now He puts the heat up so much that her impurities have to melt and her evil deposits get burned away.

Scripture Reference	Acts or Dramas	Interpretation
Ezekiel 24:15–27	Ezekiel's wife dies. He is not allowed to mourn outwardly or go through any of the mourners' customs.	Jerusalem will be destroyed and the people will not be allowed to mourn, but only groan among themselves. Ezekiel will open his mouth once the message of the destruction has been delivered.
Ezekiel 37:4–10	Ezekiel prophesies to the dry bones.	They rise up and become an army.
Ezekiel 37:15–28	Ezekiel takes a stick and writes 'Belonging to Judah and the Israelites associated with him' on it. He takes a second stick and writes 'Belonging to Joseph (that is, to Ephraim) and all the Israelites associated with him'. He puts the two sticks together to make them one stick in his hand.	God will make the two one in His hand. He will bring the people back from the lands where He scattered them and bring them back into their land. They will be one kingdom under one king. God will forgive them and cleanse them. He will be their God and they will be His people.
Hosea 1:2	Hosea marries a prostitute.	Israel is unfaithful to the Lord.
Hosea 1:3–5	Hosea's first son is called Jezreel.	God will put an end to the Kingdom of Israel in the Valley of Jezreel.

Scripture Reference	Acts or Dramas	Interpretation
Hosea 1:6–7	Hosea's first daughter is called Lo-Ruhamah.	The name means not loved. God will no longer show love to Israel, but to Judah.
Hosea 1:8–9	Hosea's second son is called Lo-Ammi.	The name means not my people because God declares that Israel is no longer His people and He is no longer her God.
Hosea 3:1–2	Hosea buys back his wife.	God will forgive Israel and take her back into covenant.
Zechariah 6:9–15	Zechariah has a crown made and puts it on the high priest Joshua.	It speaks of Jesus rebuilding the temple.
Matthew 21:12–13 See also Mark 11:15–19, Luke 19:45–48 and John 2:13–16	Jesus cleanses the Temple.	He fulfils the word in Isaiah 56:7, 'a house of prayer for all nations', in Jeremiah 7:11, 'a den of robbers', and in Malachi 3:1, 'the Lord you seek will suddenly come to his temple.'
Matthew 21:33–46 See also Mark 12:1–12 and Luke 20:9–19	The parable of the wicked vinedressers.	God is the landowner of the vineyard.

Scripture Reference	Acts or Dramas	Interpretation
Matthew 21:33–46 (*continued*)	The vineyard has a hedge and a watchtower.	Israel is the vineyard with the law as the hedge and the prophets as the watchtower.
	The owner leases the vineyard to vinedressers.	God puts authorities over Israel to help her follow Him in the covenant.
	The owner goes to a far country (long absence).	The glory or presence of God departed from Israel, Ichabod.
	Two sets of the owners' servants.	God sent prophets to the Israelites.
	The owner sends His son, but the vinedressers cast him out of the vineyard and kill him.	Jesus came but Israel did not receive Him. He died on the cross for us.
	God will lease His vineyard to other vinedressers who will give to Him the fruits in their season.	The one new man will bring in the kingdom of God and be involved in the harvest of souls.

Scripture Reference	Acts or Dramas	Interpretation
Matthew 26:17–30 See also Mark 14:12–26 and Luke 22:7–23	The Last Supper	The eating of the bread and the drinking of the third cup turn into a prophetic act of liberation and salvation in Jesus' death. Jesus establishes the New Covenant.
Luke 7:36–39 and 44–50	A woman who is a sinner washes Jesus' feet with her hair and anoints His feet with fragrant oil.	The act of submission and adorations leads Jesus to say that her sins are forgiven.
John 12:1–8 See also Matthew 26:6–13 and Mark 14:3–9	Mary, sister of Martha and Lazarus, anoints Jesus' feet with costly oil.	A foretelling of His burial (verse 7).
John 12:12–19	Jesus rides into Jerusalem on the colt of a donkey.	Fulfilment of the prophecies in Genesis 49:10–11 and Zechariah 9:9–13: He is the king who is prophesied to Zion in the Old Testament.
Acts 21:10–11	Agabus takes Paul's belt and ties his own hands and feet with it.	It symbolizes the way the Jews in Jerusalem will bind Paul and deliver him to the Gentiles.

Appendix 5 — The symbolic Foods and Rituals at the Passover Seder

Symbolic Foods	Meaning
The roasted lamb shankbone	It symbolizes the lamb eaten during the night in which the angel of death went through Egypt. It can also symbolize the arm of God as the Hebrew term *zeroah*, which means shankbone, can also mean arm. It is not eaten.
The roasted egg	It symbolizes spring time or renewal. It is not eaten.
The bitter herbs	They bring tears to the eyes (like horseradish, if used) and speak of the bitterness of the slavery in Egypt. Participants are challenged to see their own enslavement as habits and addictions. The herbs are called *maror* and get dipped into the salt water. They can also get dipped into the sweet salad. They can be made into a small sandwich, called the hallel sandwich or the *korekh*, with the sweet salad and the unleavened bread. The second bitter herb is called *chazeret*. Romaine lettuce is often used to symbolize that Jewish life in Egypt began softly and ended hard and bitter (like the two ends of this type of lettuce).
The sweet salad of apples, nuts, wine and cinnamon	It represents the mortar used to make the bricks in Egypt. Figs and dates also get used. It is called *charoset*.

Symbolic Foods	Meaning
The green vegetables	Parsley is often used. It speaks of the freshness of spring. They are called *karpas*. These foods are usually on the seder plate.
The salt water	It symbolizes the tears and sweat of slavery, but also purification.
The unleavened bread	Three pieces of it are on a plate on the table, usually covered with a cloth. The three pieces are said to represent the priests, the Levites and the rest of the Jews. Some families add a fourth piece to remember the Jews who are not able to celebrate Passover. The bread is called matzah. One piece of matzah gets broken and one half is being hidden. It is called the *afikomen*.
The four cups of wine	They stand for the biblical promises of redemption: (1) 'I will bring you out from under the burdens of the Egyptians' (2) 'I will rid you from their slavery' (3) 'I will redeem you with an outstretched arm and with great judgements' (4) 'I will take you to me for a people' Other interpretations say the cups stand for the four letters of YHWH. According to Haggadah, the first cup is for sanctification, called Kiddush; the second cup is for the narrating of the story, called Maggid; the third cup is for the grace after meals, called Birkat Hamazon; the fourth cup is for the citation of the Great Hallel, Psalm 113–118.

Rituals	Meaning
The washing of hands	Ritual purification
No blessing is spoken after the hand washing	This is done to alert the children to ask about the differences to other meal celebrations.
Breaking the bread without saying a blessing over it	This is done to alert the children to ask about the differences to other meal celebrations.
The children ask four questions about the differences to other meal celebrations. The questions are asked before the story of the Passover is retold.	There are four differences: (1) They eat unleavened bread instead of leavened bread. (2) They eat bitter herbs. (3) They dip the herbs twice. (4) The participants recline instead of eating sitting up straight. The main portion of the Seder reading leads through the answers to these questions. Someone might physically act out the retelling of the story. The four questions are answered during the reading: (1) We eat only unleavened bread because our ancestor could not wait for their breads to rise when they were fleeing slavery in Egypt, and so they were flat when they came out of the oven. (2) We eat only a bitter herb to remind us of the bitterness of slavery that our ancestors endured while in Egypt. (3) The first dip, in salt water, symbolizes the replacing of our tears with gratitude, and the second dip, in *charoset*, symbolizes the sweetening of our burden of bitterness and suffering.

Rituals	Meaning
The children ask four questions… (*continued*)	(4) We recline at the Seder table, because in ancient times, a person who reclined at a meal was a free person, while slaves and servants stood.
The hidden matzah	Either the children search for it at the time of dessert and receive a treat when they find it, or the children hide it for the parents to search. If the parents give up the search, the children receive a treat for revealing the hiding place.
	It is the last thing eaten.
A door is opened for the prophet Elijah to return and the fourth cup is poured.	This speaks of the change from reminiscing past redemption to anticipating future redemption. Elijah will be the forerunner of the Messiah.

Appendix 6 — Scripture Index

book. *Biblical Foundations of Prophetic Art* should be required reading for all students of the prophetic, for those who seek Biblical support for the arts, and for clergy who want to host the creative within the body of Christ. I found it thrilling. Yippee, Amen and Hallelujah!!!

Latimer Bowen, Abilene, USA
Prophetic artist, founder of Project 7 Billion
www.project7billion.org, facebook.com/project7billion

For years I have observed Jörn and his passion for art. Simply by his lifestyle, how he walks, how he dresses, and how he speaks cries out, "Passionate Creative!" His desire for excellence in himself and his family, as well as empowering the Body of Christ to excellence is a precious example to follow. Watching Jörn paint or create is an art in itself. His motion, his intensity and tenacity are something inspiring as well. This book: *Biblical Foundations of Prophetic Art: Finding Keys in Scripture* is really a reflection of his own life over the years and his own journey of learning what it means to be a 'prophetic artist'. I highly recommend it for those who are either discovering the value of art and their role in it, or for those mature artists who have found themselves a bit dried up in their creative process - this will definitely re-inspire and re-fire you to step back into the passion God has given to you to create.

I really enjoyed the chapter on Prophetic Writing — it touched me personally. 'What do you read on your heart when you create? In Ezekiel 9:4 the answer to this question was a matter of life and death. Is there anything you need to do about this?' Those words spoke to me right where I am and what I am doing now.

Thank you, Jörn, for taking the time, energy and resources to compile this biblically-grounded book that will release many creatives into their destiny.

Teresa Craig, Jerusalem, Israel
Writer and Photographer
www.focusedonthenations.com

I was truly blessed by Jörn's book on prophetic artists and pray that this book will find its way into the homes of artists around the world, not just to sit on a shelf, but to become an essential tool for artists of all types. I love how Jörn expounded on Zechariah 1:17-21 as I have often spoken this word over artists who feel their artwork is worthless. It's really quite amazing when you ponder this, that God would prefer to send artists with our voices, instruments, paintbrushes, bodies, etc. into the front lines of battle. You would think that He would send mighty warriors armed for battle who are highly trained and full of physical strength. But instead He chooses little Davids with harps and sling stones! May Jörn's book become a handbook for the *Sayeret Golani*, Special Forces, who are the prophetic artists of the God of Israel!

Carolyn Hyde, Galilee, Israel
Worshipper and tour group hostess
www.heartofg-d.org

Jörn's book will unify artists across continents and is a mandate toward a greater Kingdom vision for Prophetic Art. It is revelatory and articulates the Biblical foundations of Prophetic Art with both Hebrew and Greek translations. The reader gains an even greater depth of understanding, making it a vital resource for helping artists to be more strategic and effective when presenting or sharing what God is speaking through their art and creative expressions. The book is aligned with the times and seasons of God and will inspire artists both young and old to pursue the wonder of partnering with God in the creative process, and to share what He is speaking with more boldness and confidence in their spheres of influence.

Lisa Kidd, Greensboro, North Carolina, USA
Founder of Arts Evangelica
www.artsevangelica.org, facebook.com/artsevangelica

Jörn Lange has done an excellent job in researching the Biblical foundations for prophetic art. It's a rich, dense treatment of why we create under the prophetic anointing of the Holy Spirit. I encourage you to take the time to consume the important material in this book. This book meets a real need.

Prophetic art continues to spread around the world. It has been an amazing story. Like all movements, this one is growing and changing. I am so excited to see men and women not only painting in churches during worship. God is teaching us how to apply the prophetic to all areas of creative expression. We are seeing prophetic artists design animated billboards for Time Square in New York City, and others are entering the video game industry. Still others have entered the fashion and design industries, believing God has something better than the way things are. The prophetic is about making heaven visible in the earth.

From here, anything is possible.

Christ John Otto, London, United Kingdom
Director, Belonging House
Author of An Army Arising: *Why Artists are on the Front Line of the Next Move of God* and of the upcoming *Visible Image: Bezalel the Artist in the Kingdom of God*
He writes a weekly blog that is available through belonginghouse.org.

Jörn lays a biblical foundation of what prophetic art is throughout the Bible. He unlocks new perspectives on the multifaceted expression of arts throughout scripture, including creative writing, painting, singing, dancing, metal work, movement, and other forms. If you are still discovering a passion for prophetic art, this book will set a groundwork for you to build from. Our Creator God has called us to enter into the story of creating with a declaration of His Voice. As artists, we must continually lift up our eyes to the first creator-artist God, and as we do so, that which we create becomes a prophetic testimony of Jesus.

Jonathan Voge, Larnaca, Cyprus
Elder of Youth With A Mission Cyprus

It is such an honour to recommend this book. We live in times where God is restoring the artists and artisans to the church in order to release them into society with a powerful mandate of transformation. This amazing book is a great toolbox for churches and ministry leaders to have a biblical understanding of why we need to invite the artisans to seek and worship God in the Spirit; to understand their creative expression; to know how creative God is and how full of creative expressions the Bible is. This is a much needed book to give more understanding about the importance and the power art has to release the heart of the Father for this world. A piece of art can go everywhere and release His goodness. A great foundational book for everyone because in each of our lives there is a creative expression that reveals aspects of our God.

Mayra Pankow , Duisburg, Germany
Artist and mentor for prophetic artists
Leader of prophetic creative expressions,
Christus Gemeinde Duisburg, Germany
Founder of European Academy of the Arts,
Transforming Arts Movement and
European Network of Prophetic Artists.

Recently I was invited to join a panel discussion at a Creativity Summit, and in preparing I came across Jörn's first book again: *Intercession through Creative Expression* - an inspiring text laying the foundation for understanding the dynamics of creativity and the arts, explaining how the creative flow can draw heaven to earth.

What a joy it is now to have his second work in hands: *Biblical Foundations of Prophetic Art. Finding Keys in Scripture* — a comprehensive study of creative expressions and their prophetic strength.

The book starts with a closer look at God's character as the One who creates, the biblical concept of beauty and creation as divine artwork. After explaining the prophetic dimension of the arts he defines the identity and role of artists as partners with God: they make people see (seeing in a wider sense)! And then Jörn takes his readers on a tour introducing areas of human culture where we encounter expressions of prophetic art — in dance, garments and banners, music, paintings and colours, carving, engraving, sculptural artwork and pottery, prophetic writing and poetry, drama and sign action. A whole world opening up!

Jörn succeeds to lay a biblical foundation for each topic including word studies of the original languages. In opening the wide field of ways to express creativity and to become personally involved in creative work, he challenges us to leave the status quo as a viewer only, but to become a doer also. Now the keys for prophetic art literally lie in the readers' hands.

A must read for leaders who are challenged to pastor the prophetic. A must read for all who long for a release of Kingdom culture in today's society.

Klaus-Dieter Passon, Düsseldorf, Germany
Pastor of JESUS-HAUS Gemeinde

Jörn has done an excellent job with this book. *Biblical Foundations of Prophetic Art* is the most comprehensive book I have read on this topic and it reveals valuable insights into what prophetic art is, where we find it in the Bible and how art is still relevant today.

It is a must-read for artists, church leaders and those wanting to understand and support the arts. Its pages are filled with inspiring stories of past and present-day artists that have and are boldly stepping out, using their arts not only as a weapon against injustice but as a powerful tool to bring about change and reconciliation.

As a designer and art coach I will be recommending this book to my students as a go-to reference to reinforce the importance of their vocation as artists and as a source of encouragement as they are called to create.

Sonja Smalheer, Barn, The Netherlands
Art coach & podcaster
www.sonjasmalheer.com

A few years ago I met Jörn at an art exhibition. We served people side by side with our fast and simple sketches and paintings. His passion for people and his joy in creative pursuit find their expression in the lines of this book. This book is a valuable, biblically anchored companion for creative people who desire to unite spirituality and creativity; for readers who want to encounter God as an artist and to learn more about His creativity. It is a book which is to be cherished and enjoyed slowly in order to gain the maximum benefit from it. Jörn combines the common idioms and artistic expressions with an in-depth examination of the biblical texts. How valuable it is when Spirit and word — rhema and logos — come together and create active faith as creative everyday life results from them.

Ruth Truttmann, Aarau, Switzerland
Ruth studied theology and is a freelance artist and the leader of the
Prophetic Arts at FCG Aarau, Switzerland
Founder of visual-voice.ch